the art of john cederquist
REALITY OF ILLUSION

arthur c. danto

nancy princenthal

introduction by

kenneth r. trapp

oakland museum of california

This publication, and the exhibition
it accompanies, has been supported by
a grant from the National Endowment
for the Arts.

exhibition schedule

Oakland Museum of California
13 September–30 November 1997

Renwick Gallery
of the National Museum of American Art
Smithsonian Institution, Washington, D.C.
24 September 1999–9 January 2000

Exhibition curator:
Kathy L. Borgogno

Catalogue editor:
Fronia W. Simpson

Catalogue designer:
Barbara Ziller

Cover designer:
Andrew Richards,
Barbara Ziller Graphic Design, Inc.
San Francisco, California 94102

Printed in Hong Kong through
Global Interprint

Apart from the exceptions noted,
photographs of Cederquist's work:
Michael A. Sasso

Robert Hashimoto, Pl. 12
Ron Leighton, p. 16
John Patrick Salisbury, p. 128
Joe Samberg, p. 7
Evan Sheppard, Pls. 36, 44, p. 4
Ole Woldbye, Pl. 31

Library of Congress
Catalog Card No. 97-065870

ISBN 1-882140-17-6 Hardback
ISBN 1-882140-16-8 Paperback

contents

5

foreword
Dennis M. Power

6

acknowledgments
John Cederquist

7

introduction
Kenneth R. Trapp

10

illusion and comedy:
the art of john cederquist
Arthur C. Danto

20

john cederquist:
theater in the round
Nancy Princenthal

28

plates

128

biography
Kate Rothrock

132

selected bibliography
Kate Rothrock

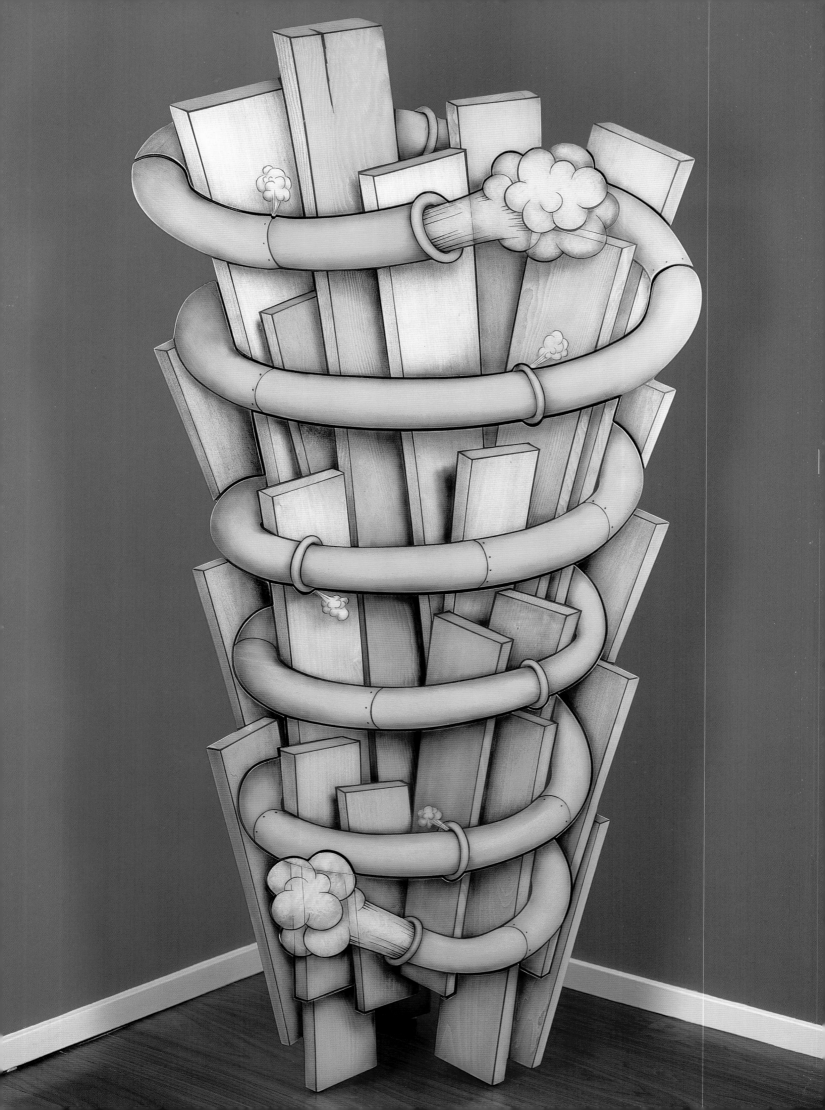

foreword

The art of John Cederquist is a treat. I have read that his work "challenges all perceptions of its beholder as to the very meaning of orientation." I am glad that Cederquist's art bears serious scrutiny, but to me it is just wonderful "fun." Perhaps because we were both brought up in Southern California, I find in his art a commonality of response to pale wood (sun bleached?), false-perspective movie sets, waves from the Pacific Rim, and cartoons.

Exploring the body of work in the exhibition *The Art of John Cederquist: Reality of Illusion,* we might think of a continuum along which we have "furniture" at one extreme, "functional art" in the middle, and "art" at the other end. Because his work is functional we want to characterize it as furniture. It is furniture, but even more it is art. It is also finely crafted functional art, but the problem here may be that it does not look functional. So, what are we left with: a new category? How about "surreal domicile *meuble*"? As I said, it's fun.

I have seen the movie *Roger Rabbit* discussed in writings about John Cederquist. I like that: a comedy/thriller that mixed real actors and animated characters in a Southern California setting. Like a favorite cartoon, much of his work is downright lovable.

Who do we have to thank for bringing us the harmonious disharmony seen in the exhibition and this catalogue? Franklin Parrasch of the Franklin Parrasch Gallery in New York has been extremely helpful in finding lenders and collections to draw from. His support is sincerely appreciated. The idea for this exhibition is credited to Kenneth R. Trapp, formerly associate curator at our museum and now curator-in-charge of the Renwick Gallery, National Museum of American Art, Smithsonian Institution. It was left to curatorial specialist Kathy L. Borgogno to bring the exhibition and publication to fruition, and she did it as usual—reliably and competently. Special thanks also to editor Fronia W. Simpson and book designer Barbara Ziller. We gratefully acknowledge financial support from the National Endowment for the Arts, the general operating budget of the Oakland Museum of California Foundation, and the Oakland Museum Women's Board.

Dennis M. Power
Executive Director

steamer chest, 1993
Baltic birch plywood, poplar, nutmeg, maple,
Sitka spruce, epoxy resin inlay, aniline dye
68 x 34 x 14 inches
Collection of Robert and Toni Gordon

acknowledgments

I would like to thank the Oakland Museum of California, the National Endowment for the Arts, and the Oakland Museum Women's Board for their support in making this exhibition possible. With constant and increasing reductions in both state and federal funding, I am exceedingly grateful for this opportunity to exhibit my work.

Watching the project evolve was quite a learning experience. For my part, I soon realized that the making of an exhibition is a complete contrast to the independence and isolation of my studio. I also realized that I was completely dependent on the diverse talents of museum curators and directors, design professionals, old friends, and total strangers. I would therefore like to thank and acknowledge them all for their efforts in making this project the success that it is.

Without Ken Trapp's vision, commitment, fortitude, and ingenuity, *The Art of John Cederquist: Reality of Illusion* would not exist. Although Ken left the museum for new challenges at the Renwick, it is fitting that he could return to the project and contribute to it his fine introduction.

For me, Ken's departure left a vacuum of uncertainty, but any anxieties I had over the fate of the exhibition quickly vanished after my first phone conversation with the new curator-in-charge. Kathy Borgogno's curatorial skills left me with no doubts as to the project's timely realization.

Mike Sasso's fifteen years of consistently beautiful photography were used most effectively by Barbara Ziller in her catalogue design, while Arthur Danto's and Nancy Princenthal's insightful essays made it much more than just a picture book. I would also like to thank Kate Rothrock for her patience with me in writing the biography and to Fronia Simpson for her skilled editing of the manuscript. Thanks go to those who orchestrated the installation, Ted Cohen for exhibition design, David Ruddell and the entire technical support crew for their mindfulness in handling the endless details.

Chris LaBonte has assisted me in the studio for the last eight years. His excellent craftsmanship and attention to detail have been invaluable in the making of the more recent body of work.

I would also like to thank my parents for their early support. Thanks also to my wife, Suzanne, for her patience both on the home front and in the studio, and to my daughter, Tera, for letting me watch cartoons with her on Saturday mornings.

Finally, I would like to thank the lenders and Franklin Parrasch for his assistance in gathering these pieces together, if for no other reason than to see what the last seventeen years of work look like all in one place.

John Cederquist

The Oakland Museum of California extends its sincere appreciation to the following individuals, whose generosity made this catalogue possible:

John W. and Marilyn L. Barrett
Daphne Farago
Diane and Marc Grainer
Franklin and Suzi Parrasch
Carolyn J. and Robert C. Springborn
Charles and Mapes Stamm

introduction

The Art of John Cederquist: Reality of Illusion is the first museum exhibition devoted to the compelling constructions of John Cederquist. By presenting here some forty pieces made by Cederquist between 1981 and 1997, the Oakland Museum of California pays tribute to a native son of the Golden State whose creative imagination far transcends arbitrary boundaries of classification.

John Cederquist is not a celebrity whose name is known far and wide in American households. Who is John Cederquist? Of his many aspects, I will look at Cederquist the Californian, Cederquist the aging baby boomer now past his half-century mark, and Cederquist the artist. The first two aspects of Cederquist's life inform the third.

Born in Altadena in Los Angeles County, John Cederquist entered the exclusive club of those who proclaim themselves native Californians. Although such a jealously guarded birthright may strike other Americans as odd, native Californians often seem to regard themselves as almost incidentally American.

But more to the point, Cederquist is not just a Californian but a Southern Californian. The distinction is measured in attitude rather than in miles. Northern and Southern California are distinct regions, poles apart in their historical and cultural evolution and in the carefully nurtured self-perceptions of their citizens.

For more than fifty years Cederquist has lived in Southern California. For that fact to escape expression in his art would hardly be possible. Steeped in the Southern California life-cum-mythology, Cederquist's art bears witness to specific place in both overt and subtle ways.

"Being a Californian gave me permission to do the California thing," Cederquist notes without irony. California offered two advantages for a young man entering the world of art. Clinging to the continent on the Pacific West Coast, California was far removed from the populated eastern United States, which had long molded American culture and defined the mainstream of the visual arts. California's isolation—as much psychological as physical—fostered an independence of mind and the attitude that anything is possible, especially in spite of tradition.

Second, when Cederquist took his first step into art, California had no long-established history in craft. Had he wanted to study furniture design and furniture making in California in the 1960s, Cederquist would have had a hard time finding a mentor or a program. The lack of a strong craft tradition in California was itself an encouragement for the artist to experiment. Cederquist's education in the liberal arts was the antithesis of an apprenticeship in a practical trade.

California is the inspiration for some of Cederquist's imagery. Describing himself as the stereotypical "laid-back surfer," Cederquist bows to his beach-boy youth in *Tubular*, a spectacular tribute to the Japanese artist Hokusai's famous *Great Wave at Kanagawa* from the series *Thirty-six Views of Fuji* of the 1820s. In surfer lingo, "tubular" is the perfect rolling wave that forms a spiraling tube. Hence, "totally tubular" is a metaphor for the ultimate, purest experience.

Surfing is but one California passion that serves to define John Cederquist. He is a child of the sixties steeped in the urban lore of Southern California replete with Beach Boys tunes, hot rods, Disneyland, and living free in some kind of paradise. But this seemingly idyllic upbringing is thrown into high relief by a different reality. Cederquist came of age in the tumultuous time of Cold War politics, television, rock 'n' roll, human rights struggles, Vietnam, drop-out, drop-acid hippies, and the Love generation.

If place is important in Cederquist's evolution as an artist, then the time in which he reached his majority is equally significant. Cederquist was born in 1946, the first of eighteen years that encompass what has come to be called the Baby Boom generation. The first generation born immediately after World War II, the baby boomers enjoyed privileges of comforts, luxuries, and opportunities that their parents never dreamed of during the back-to-back calamities of the Great Depression and World War II.

Cederquist's life to date parallels the evolution of the contemporary studio craft movement in America. He entered college at an age when previous generations of his family had to work. In college he studied art and eventually found his calling in craft. It was Cederquist's great good fortune to be born in California just as the state began to create the most progressive higher education system in the world to accommodate an exploding population. And it was within that system, at Long Beach State College (now California State University, Long Beach), that he began to shape his career.

With tongue-in-cheek humor, Cederquist makes sport of slaying sacred cows. A revered dictum of twentieth-century design is "Form follows function." Cederquist consciously and deliberately perverts this dictum to achieve his artistic aim. His constructions are not really about form so much as they are about image. In fact, form is incidental to the overriding interest in imagery. Cederquist maintains that his furniture is functional, but it is functional in the same way that a fifteen-pound cast-iron teakettle or a dull knife is functional—hardly.

Cederquist argues that for him "form follows function" is an incomplete statement because it fails to take into account the importance of imagery. And it is here that Cederquist parts company with his colleagues who create fully functional furniture. To study Cederquist's art at any length is to understand his impulse.

Cederquist is not a furniture maker, a fact evident to even the casual viewer, and a fact that the artist himself acknowledges. He is not a master woodcarver, woodturner, furniture designer, or wood expert and technician. Cederquist is not interested in these aspects of wood. Further, Cederquist is essentially indifferent to form. The suggestion of furniture in Cederquist's art is often not in the forms of his pieces but in the imagery of furniture parts—legs, a broken pediment, finials—he paints on his forms. In *The Missing Finial,* for example, the image of a leg is superimposed on a leg itself—the image of the leg reinforces the structure of a leg.

In some instances Cederquist makes light of hallowed furniture design in the United States. He is fond of the stately colonial American high chest, with its classic broken pediment crest and turned finials, and he uses this imagery in his masterworks *The Missing Finial* and *Ghost Boy.*

With ironic twists, Cederquist pays homage to past furniture tradition at the same time as he freely interprets his chosen images from that tradition. His art is often about art and only coincidentally about form. In *The Missing Finial* and *Ghost Boy* there is a sense of a modern master painter at work. The fracturing of the imagery and the reduced, subdued palette bring to mind the cubism of Picasso and Braque, as Cederquist is quick to acknowledge.

It is not within the scope of this introduction to discuss in detail the wealth of imagery in Cederquist's artistic vocabulary. Suffice it to say that it is impossible to overestimate the importance of imagery to Cederquist. He is consumed with appearance, with surface. Like the first radio generation, those of us who were the first television generation recall the influence of that electronic medium on our lives. Cederquist is no exception. Indeed, for him television is a constant source of imagery, an ever-changing encyclopedia of new pictures. Perhaps this element of his art brings him most solidly and clearly back to California. In a land with few traditions with which to anchor one's life, and in a place where illusion assumes the substance of reality, Cederquist has found his voice. And an eloquent voice it is.

Those who mistake Cederquist's humor for frivolity will miss his pointed message: image is content. Some might think there is *less* than meets the eye in Cederquist's fascination with illusionistic effects, but when I look at the art of John Cederquist, I am reminded of the adage, "To think of nothing is not the same as not thinking." Cederquist creates art for the thinking person.

Kenneth R. Trapp
Curator-in-Charge
Renwick Gallery, National Museum of American Art
Smithsonian Institution

illusion and comedy: the art of john cederquist

Arthur C. Danto

Thus trompe-l'oeil transcends painting. It is a kind of game with reality which, since the sixteenth century, takes on fantastic dimensions and ends by removing the divisions between painting, sculpture, and architecture.

— Jean Baudrillard, "The Trompe-l'oeil"

fig. 1

Baudrillard's essay on trompe l'oeil originally appeared in *Signs of Change: A Reader in Applied Semiotics*, sponsored by the International Center of Semiotics and Linguistics at the University of Urbino, and it makes explicit reference to one of the most spectacular examples of trompe-l'oeil art, the celebrated studiolo, traditionally attributed to Sandro Botticelli and Baccio Pintelli, in Urbino's own Palazzo Ducale. The studiolo of Urbino, like its counterpart, the studiolo of Gubbio (which is now permanently installed in the Metropolitan Museum of Art in New York), was created for the great general Federico da Montefeltro, and both these works indeed transcend the conventional divisions between painting, architecture, and sculpture. They belong to architecture by virtue of the fact that they are, after all, rooms; they belong to painting in that each creates illusions of depth by applying the principles of perspective discovered shortly beforehand by Filippo Brunelleschi; and they belong to sculpture by virtue of the fact that the rooms' walls are produced by the ingenious fitting together of thousands of pieces of shaped wood, creating the illusion of books, of military gear, and of musical and scientific instruments, arrayed in cupboards with opened doors in latticework. There appear to be, as well, items of furniture—benches and lecterns—three-dimensional to vision, two-dimensional to touch, placed around the lower register of the mysterious spaces, and, in the cupboard nearest the window in the Gubbio studiolo, a somewhat less than convincing parrot in a cage. (It is not altogether easy to depict a parrot in linear perspective.) The placing of the ducal helmet and armor together with the books, the lute and harp, the writing instruments, the armillary and the quadrant declares that there is an art of war as of poetry, music, and mathematics. The room itself proclaims the arts of architecture, sculpture, and painting as well as the art of intarsia, which makes possible this great exemplar of the Renaissance spirit in the medium of cut and stained wood. A game is certainly played between the actual and the illusory space, light, and shadows of the duke's inner chamber (fig. 1).

John Cederquist's works also are games played with actual and apparent light, shadow, and space, and they resemble the studioli of Urbino and Gubbio through the fact that they, too, remove the divisions between painting, sculpture, and—in place of architecture—the art of furniture. The actual walls of the studioli are also pictures, in the medium of shaped and inlaid wood, which exploit the phenomenon of perspective to create the illusions of other walls. The duality between illusion and reality is ingeniously achieved through what appear to be the bottoms of some of the benches that line the walls. These are in the kind of ornamental marquetry one finds on the tops and sides of those inlaid wooden boxes to be bought in souvenir shops in Tuscany. But, since the surfaces they embellish in the studiolo are shown in perspective, the identical surface is at once an example of marquetry and a wooden picture of some marquetry. It is no mean feat to create the perspectival illusion of marquetry in the medium of marquetry itself, which makes it clear that the subtleties of the studioli were created for the pleasure of minds alive to the paradoxes of pictorial representation. That spirit of Renaissance perceptual play is reborn in Cederquist's oeuvre—the renaissance of the Renaissance—most perspicuously in his masterpiece, *Le Fleuron Manquant (The Missing Finial)* of 1989 (Pl. 13), which is an actual chest as well as a picture of a chest. The illusory chest—the one pictured on the facade of the real chest—is itself a real and indeed a famous chest, in the Museum of Fine Arts, Boston. The chest that does the picturing—Cederquist's—stands in perceptually maddening relationships to the chest pictured.

fig. 2

The Missing Finial was expressly built for the 1989 exhibition *New American Furniture*, which was originated by the Museum of Fine Arts, Boston. Furniture makers were invited to participate and charged "to take inspiration from a particular piece in the collection—whether from a decorative detail, nomenclature, or social use—and to make a new work, specifically for inclusion in this exhibition." So each work on display referred to the piece that inspired it, a fact that vested these pieces with a dimension of meaning not typically possessed by articles of furniture. But Cederquist went beyond this: *his* piece actually *pictured* its inspiration, which was a high chest, from about 1760, built by John Townsend of Newport, Rhode Island (fig. 2). It is relatively rare for a piece of furniture to be a picture, let alone a picture of another piece of furniture, and a narrative picture as well: *The Missing Finial* actually tells a story about the high chest it represents. (If the story is not true, that goes with the logic of stories and belongs to the domain of illusion.) The relationships between the real chest pictured and the real chest that pictures it are as complex as the system of perspective the latter uses to create the illusion of the former. The chest that pictures—the work titled *The Missing Finial*—is in real three-dimensional space, whereas the chest pictured in perspective, of which Cederquist is as complete a master as the designers of the studioli, is situated in a pictorial space, so that its surface is not identical with the surface of *The Missing Finial* itself, which is after all a picture plane as well as the front of the actual chest. The drawers of *The Missing Finial,* functional enough to put socks and underwear in, do not at all correspond to the drawn drawers of the illusory chest. The *spirit* of *The Missing Finial* is the spirit of the studiolo, even if—or especially because—it is also in the spirit of postmodernism, which is what allows it to exist comfortably with the past. It is striking that intarsia facilitates the same order of games with reality in postmodern as in quattrocento times.

Townsend high chest
with Cederquist overlay
sketch

Those familiar with Cederquist's work have sometimes wondered whether he needs to continue to make furniture, since the effect of his work is so pictorial: a photograph of one of his typical works can look like the reproduction of a painting—indeed, in the case of *The Missing Finial,* a cubist painting. But the works would lose a great deal more than whatever limited utility they have as chests or tables were he to concentrate merely on the facades and produce pictures in intarsia. He would lose entire dimensions of meaning, reference, and play. It would be tantamount to putting frames around the panels of the studiolo, which would, to be sure, still belong to the genre of trompe l'oeil, as do the paintings of William Michael Harnett or N. A. Brooks, and still display the virtuosity of their intarsia. But they would lose the magic they bestow upon the room they line, upon which, after all, they confer whatever *ritual* use they possessed for the duke. The images in the studioli subserve no practical use at all: the duke could not read the books or play upon the instruments or converse with the caged wooden bird. These are, as one text puts it, encomiastic emblems: they pay tribute to the military power of the person to whom they refer, as well as to his considerable humanistic culture. He would have entered the room to be surrounded by images of his glory, as the mirror of his brilliant life: there is an image of the Order of the Garter and other decorations as well. They would, together with the dazzling array of instruments and books, not to mention the ingenuity of the concept of the room, impress upon visitors in the fifteenth century an image of their host's stature—it would be a kind of *ecce homo*. Still, it is a room, with all the connotations of a private sanctuary, to which the owner might retire to contemplate his life and what gave meaning to it. As mere images, framed and hung like tapestries or paintings along a gallery wall, the pieces of intarsia would deflate into mere decoration and would

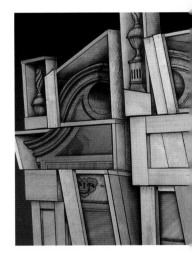

Detail, *Le Fleuron Manquant (The Missing Finial)*

Detail, *Le Fleuron Manquant (The Missing Finial)*

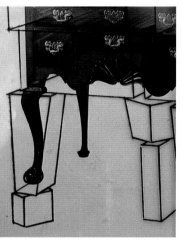

Townsend high chest with Cederquist overlay sketch

lose their entire symbolic power. Cederquist's pieces are in general done on spec, so they cannot pay tribute to their owner other than as a patron of advanced studio furniture. But they facilitate Cederquist's demonic dedication to illusion by virtue of the play they open up between what they are and what they are of. Finding where the actual drawers are in *The Missing Finial* is to overcome an obstacle everything visual about it puts in the way. The dimensions of John Townsend's chest are 87 by 39 by 20 inches; the dimensions of *The Missing Finial* are 78 by 35 by 12. Its surprising shallowness as a chest situates it in a curious space halfway between pictorial and actual space. It occupies, as Cederquist likes to say about his pieces, two-and-a-half dimensions.

Cederquist has deconstructed—a term he borrows from postmodern philosophy—Townsend's chest into its constituent parts: legs, drawers, pediment, finials. This refers to his knowledge of books, like Thomas Chippendale's *Gentleman and Cabinet Maker's Director* of 1754, which illustrated various options as to form and decoration—a bit like a book from which one can have a shirt custom-made by choosing this collar, those cuffs, that pocket. The work pictures the various parts of the chest as they might appear having arrived in individual crates that have been partly opened to reveal the part contained within. The partially opened crates are pictured as having been assembled to show the parts that have been ordered, as if to give some idea of what the assembled chest will look like. It is the deconstruction and the fictive reconstruction that lend the work its cubist feeling, enhanced by the fictive graining of the wood, which reminds us of the *faux bois* Braque and Picasso exploited in cubism's synthetic phase. The crates together with the disassembled chest pieces enable Cederquist to make an arch internal contrast between the rough carpentry involved in nailing crates together and fine cabinetry of what is after all an eighteenth-century masterpiece. It is amusing to note that the finials each have crates of their own, one of which is "empty," in reference to the eponymous missing finial.

As near as I can determine, the crate meant to hold the chest's left leg looks as empty as the crate that refers to the rightmost finial, but the work is not titled *The Missing Leg.* The title tells a story, as dramatic as stories about pieces of furniture get. A companion piece to Townsend's chest, according to Cederquist, was sent out on loan and was returned with one of its finials missing. Considering the rarity of the piece, and its appraisal in the millions of dollars, this represents an economic as well as an artistic tragedy. The piled cases thus are temporally ambiguous: we could have a representation of the component parts ordered from the *Director*, with one piece missing; or of the piece, taken apart for shipping to some other museum, and returned minus a finial, worth a lot more in the late twentieth than in the mid–eighteenth century. Either way, it is a witty idea to have built a piece of narrative furniture. The wit is carried through by displaying the crates holding the chest's left legs propped up on small boxes, made in perspective, so the chest rests *en pointe*, like a dancer. The props enable the pictured chest to be shown in perspective, and hence at an angle to the viewer who in fact stands exactly in front of it: the face of the illusory chest is in a plane different from the front of the real chest. Without props, its left legs would dangle disconcertingly in the air, destroying the illusion, instead of resting on something "solid." The "points" of the supporting boxes are orthogonal to the bottom of the right front leg, and indeed they belong to the single main plane of the facade. (In fact there are two planes, corresponding to the edge between the front and sides of the packing crates on the work's right side. The actual angle is very obtuse, whereas the angle pictured is the expected right angle. It is almost impossible, simply by looking, to determine how many planes there are.) A problem, which would have delighted a Renaissance patron of intarsia, is: where are the actual drawers? For none of the illusory drawers could be opened, not just because they are illusory but because, within the illusion, they are obstructed by part of their containing crates. But the actual drawers open with the delicious smoothness of exquisitely made furniture—when you are able to find them. The curator at the Boston exhibition, Edward S. Cooke, Jr., allowed me to open and close one.

The chest-cum-crates is shown in three-quarter view, and it is quite impossible, looking at a picture of *The Missing Finial* or, for that matter, looking at the work itself from a position in front of it, not to see *it* as if in three-quarter view. The illusion is so acute that we seem to be seeing front and side from the same perspective, at a normal right angle to one another, rather than at the fairly flat, obtuse angle touch would reveal. What seems to be the vertical edge closest to us corresponds visually to where the crates make their expected right angle in fact is nearly in the same plane as the edges that seem to be farthest away, and what seem to be regular rectangles in spatial recession are in fact irregular trapezoids and lozenges arrayed on just two flat surfaces to engender the illusion of depth, just as in the studiolo's demonic intarsia.

I asked if there were any drawing for the work, but Cederquist told me that he draws directly on the Baltic birch plywood he invariably uses as the ground for his pieces. The underdrawing defines the "inlay" shapes, which are to be formed out of different kinds of wood and fitted together, analogously to the way the sinopia, or underdrawing, of a fresco defines the array of colored shapes that constitute the surface of the finished painting. Between edge and edge of the individual pieces, Cederquist squeezes pigmented epoxy, which he then sands flush with the surfaces. The lines of epoxy constitute the surface "drawing" of the work. The surfaces of the flat pieces are stained to create the illusion of shadows: there are no real shadows in the work, any more than there are in the studiolo, where, I have read, the clever craftsmen charred the wood to create the effect of the deep shadows within the cupboards or underneath the benches. The wood grain represented is, in most cases, the actual wood grain of the inlay pieces, so that mahogany and spruce (the studiolo uses poplar and spindle wood) both are and represent mahogany and spruce. Cederquist is constantly on the lookout for woods that may serve an illusionistic purpose—maple can yield the illusion of bone, and a marvelous knot he found turned out to look like the surface pattern of a fish steak, enhancing the illusion of a handsome shark he was working into a headboard when I visited his shop, shown cut across the grain of its "flesh" (Pl. 48). For the decorative hardware of the highboy, he used koa, a Hawaiian wood, not for its beauty or its rarity, but for its reflective quality, which gave it a kinship with the original brasswork of the handles. For the saw blades, ostensibly in metal, of the *Saw Chair* (Pl. 33) the artist employed wood with a chatoyant pattern. (*Chatoyant* is a word Cederquist was astonished to find existed, and it refers to the property of having a changeable luster, like a cat's-eye gemstone.) The marvel of the saw blades is that they look like wood attempting to look like metal, exactly after the manner of the instruments in the studiolo, fusing the warmth of the one and the chill of the other, an effect one feels Cederquist must cherish. It appears, for example, in the clamminess of the fish steak fused with the warmth of the wood which creates the illusion of flesh. The wood that represents wood in *The Missing Finial* is, so to speak, self-representational, reality and simulation at once.

A great many of the illusionistic devices of *The Missing Finial* are incorporated in the 1992 *Ghost Boy*, which stars, so to speak, the same chest on chest, its full complement of finials restored (Pl. 25). *Ghost Boy* carries to a further point the cubist devices of *The Missing Finial*, and it is in consequence more pictorial than its predecessor. This turns up especially in the treatment of the pediment, which is broken up in ways that jar against the principle of "good continuity" Gestalt psychology speaks of. (Cubism too violates this principle.) In the earlier piece, the parts of the chest were distributed in integral ways among the various crates. But in *Ghost Boy*, integral parts are fragmented: the pediment "jumps," as if refracted, from one crate to the next, and certain displacements suggest that the same part appears twice. It would be exceedingly difficult to "unpack" the crates and reassemble a whole piece of furniture. The shelf on which the upper chest rests, for example, appears twice, and there are certain impossible angles in the lower set of drawers. For these reasons, there is no impulse to reach out and touch, to confirm or disconfirm what vision reveals, any more than there is with a cubist painting. There is a great deal of visual dazzle, but

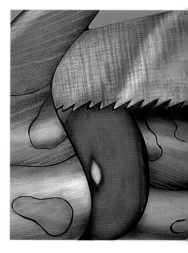

Detail, *Road to Dreamland*

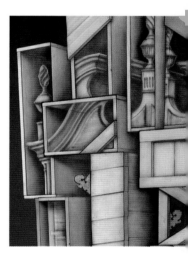

Detail, *Ghost Boy*

Lowboy

sacrificing good continuity in the interests of cubist development dissolves the effect of illusion. Of course, the subject here is a ghost, and we have little insight into the visual structure of ghosts. The term was recommended by the pickling of the wood—though some of the upper drawers are of unbleached poplar, leaving it a question of whether we are dealing with resurrection or disintegration. The title, quite legitimate if we consider the series highboy, lowboy, ghost boy, highlights the word *boy*, raising for me the question of what the term was doing in the compound word *highboy* in the first instance. (My dictionaries are mute on the etymology of the term.) The move, meanwhile, from visual illusion to visual impossibility is a development that requires an explanation. I suspect that illusionism became in some measure hostage to impossibility when Cederquist began making chests in which waves roared out of packing cases: it is not exactly obvious how to render waves in perspective, and Cederquist, moreover, employed a Japanese style for rendering water, a style that never especially aspired to illusionism. But I want to defer discussing the wave, a central motif in Cederquist's later work, until I have identified a few more elements in the artist's sensibility.

Cederquist takes a certain satisfaction in citing plywood in the list of materials for his pieces, as he does in bestowing upon the representation of packing crates the same degree of intricate craftsmanship he devotes to the simulation of rare antiques. These traits of his connect with a certain impish subversiveness in his artistic persona and belong to the same pattern as the sly way in which he *paints* a dovetail joint to mock the pieties of high-craft joinery, which has obsessed woodworkers who embrace an aesthetics of purity, analogous to that enjoined by the celebrated art critic Clement Greenberg. Each art, Greenberg wrote in his essay "Modernist Painting," "had to determine, through its own operations and works, the effects peculiar to itself." But this turned out to mean that "the unique and proper area of competence of each art coincided with all that was unique in the nature of its medium." This implied a certain critical stance: each of the arts was to be judged in terms of its degree of fidelity to its proper medium, which entailed that "each art would be rendered 'pure,' and in its 'purity' find the guarantee of its standards, of quality as well as of its independence." Greenberg wrote this in 1960, and its impact on painting is well known. Painting sought to purge itself of anything that did not belong to its essence, and this entailed a celebration of flatness—"the ineluctable flatness of the surface that remained however, more fundamental than anything else to the processes by which pictorial art flourished and defined itself under Modernism." It is as though Cederquist decided that since painting had no further use for perspective, or for the illusionistic space that underlay the need for its discovery, he would simply borrow it for purposes of furniture making, while at the same time use craft to mock craft, opposing in the true spirit of *post*modernism the commitment to a purity of joinery and veneer that was taken to be that which in woodworking was "peculiar to itself." In no sense is Cederquist interested in purity, and the razzle of illusionism in his furniture is a strategy of undermining the modernist classification of the arts. Cederquist's anarchism goes further even than this: he scorned the distinction between fine and popular art (what Greenberg dismisses as "kitsch" in a famous essay) by drawing his inspiration from cartoons. In truth, it would be Popeye quite as much as Piero della Francesca he might cite were he pressed for his chief inspiration—though Piero, like Cederquist, was mad on the subject of perspective and wrote a theoretical text dedicated to geometry and visual perception, *De prospectiva pingendi*. The final ironism worth noting—and what endears his work to me—is the way Cederquist infuses what is after all an item of high luxury with low comedy. As he said to me in his wry, direct way, "Who would want to pay fifty thousand dollars for a clown car?" There are other dimensions to his insurrection, but let us pause and deal with these before moving on.

Cederquist is the product of the graduate program in crafts at Long Beach State (now California State University, Long Beach), and not long after earning his master's degree, he found a position in the art department of Saddleback College, a community college in Orange County. This is not altogether the curriculum vitae of someone destined for greatness in the visual arts, and it is rendered further inauspicious through the fact that his immediate specialty was "leather forming." Whatever one thinks of the division between art and craft, leather forming would seem unambiguously a craft since one would be hard-pressed to identify a major work of art that belongs to the genre. Cellini was a metalworker, and Raphael could be reckoned a fiber artist through the circumstance of having drawn the cartoons for the great suite of tapestries known as *The Acts of the Apostles*. Meret Oppenheim gained a kind of immortality by covering a cup, saucer, and spoon in fur, but it was the idea rather than the exercise of craft that gave the work its celebrity. Leatherwork seems to have an auxiliary role in art through bookbinding or tooled furniture or wall coverings but not to have special claim to art in its own right, though lately, because of its ritual association with sadomasochist practices, it has gained entry into the materials of the artist in Nancy Grossman's scary hoods, with zippered eye and mouth openings. Mostly, however, leather forming has been applied to objects of either extreme utility or high luxury, but except in cases such as Grossman's it has not had associated with it the kinds of meaning that might transform objects made of leather into works of art. Cederquist might thus have lived out his life as a little-known figure in a marginal field of art, making his living by teaching graphic design in an obscure college. Linear perspective, which was central to his syllabus, would seem to have had implications for the practice of art nearly as minimal as those of leather forming. In an art world whose agenda was defined by Greenbergian principles, there was no critical space for illusionism in painting. Neither the study of perspective nor the craft of leather forming would seem to have promised much by way of distinction in an artistic career. There is a very weak determinism for artistic destiny: Warhol designed shoe ads, Johns and Rauschenberg did windows for Tiffany's, de Kooning painted signs. But these figures were parts of groups, with a vivid sense of where art was heading, and they, after all, worked in New York City, where the frontiers of art are never far away. But Cederquist seems to have been an artistic loner, in the least avant-garde milieu imaginable: Orange County is a world of rock-ribbed conservatives and beach boys. Probably all this was a blessing. It enabled the artist to find a way altogether his own.

An early work, humble enough in scale by contrast with *The Missing Finial*, exhibits Cederquist's originality and indeed his quirkiness as an artistic thinker. And it implies a methodology that was to lead to the curious and captivating trompe-l'oeil furniture which is the subject of the present exhibition. The work consists of a pair of shoes, beautifully crafted but clunky and comical, which could belong to no one in the world but Olive Oyl, as every reader of *Popeye* would immediately perceive. To add to the humor and make a point about Olive's dowdy gracelessness, *Olive's Shoes*, as the work is called, consists of two right shoes (fig. 3). It was a brilliant idea to transform an emblematic piece of footwear from the two-dimensional world of *Thimble Theater* into a three-dimensional sculpture in the appropriate medium of leather, and it was that transformation rather than the shoes as such that proved to be the fulcrum for Cederquist's vision. There was a pair of Mickey's shoes—I suppose in yellow leather —and there could, had the artist cared to pursue this vein, have been a pair of Vincent's shoes, a sculptural rendition of those profoundly moving shoes of which Heidegger made so much in his great essay, "The Origin of the Artwork." But this was not a deep vein of artistic possibility, any more than Popeye's hat would have been if executed by a fiber artist. It was, as it turned out, the preoccupation with the relationship between two- and three-dimensional representation—the domain to which perspective holds the key—that put Cederquist on the path to the furniture pieces. They were, so to speak, three-dimensional two-dimensional objects, like cartoon figures brought to life, existing as two-dimensional beings in a three-dimensional world like Roger Rabbit, as Ronald Jones and Franklin Parrasch have noted in their essays on the artist. In fact, the combination of animated and real figures belongs to the earliest days of animation, when Max Fleischer would draw Koko the Clown coming out of a real ink bottle and have him cavort on the drawing board, interacting with Fleischer himself, diverting the film audience with the impression that a drawn figure had been

fig. 3

fig. 4

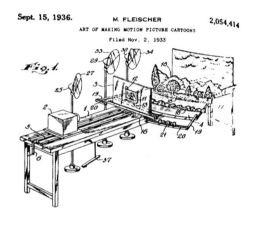

fig. 5

fig. 6

brought to life! Olive's Chair, the first of these works, belongs to this hybrid order for which we have already used Cederquist's term—a two-and-a-half-dimensional object (Pl. 4). It is striking that one of the great works on computational optics, *Vision: A Computational Investigation* (1982) by David Marr, should have arrived at this identical curious quantity—two-and-a-half dimensions—to characterize the dimensionality of retinal images.

A good but inadvertent example of a three-dimensional two-dimensional object was brought to my attention through an anecdote told me by the sculptor Brian Nissen, who spends a certain portion of each year working in Mexico. Nissen needed a table built by a carpenter he employed from time to time, and on this occasion, he drew it in perspective. Much to his surprise he found that the carpenter had *built* the table in perspective, that is, as an irregular parallelogram! This would be analogous to someone laying railroads tracks in such a way that they met, translating an optical phenomenon into a physical one. The idea of drawing a table with built-in perspective would present a terrific challenge to a Renaissance artist like Piero della Francesca—or Paolo Uccello—who enjoyed opportunities to display virtuosity. There is in the Gubbio studiolo, for example, a ring with octagonal cross sections, known as a *mazzocchio,* of which a perspective rendering by Piero exists (fig. 4). *Olive's Chair* is the reverse of a perspective drawing: it is the realization in three dimensions of a chair originally in cartoon perspective, in which the chair retains its perspectivity when given the dimensionality that descends upon drawn objects when brought into our world, out of one medium into another, like a fish wrenched from water into air. The chair in this instance comes from Olive Oyl's parlor, the arena in which her suitors, Popeye and Bluto, ritually battle for the dowdy lady's skinny favors.

Cederquist recalls watching cartoons on Saturday mornings with his daughter when she was little and finding that he was becoming interested in the way the animation studio handled spatial relationships between characters and background objects. These would have been Max Fleischer's ingenious "setbacks," which he used to great effect in the *Popeye* cartoons (fig. 5). They consisted of scenery drawn (usually) in the same style as the characters but mounted on a rotating stage, which moved a fraction of an inch with each change of cel. The cel would be hung in front of the camera, and the figure was opaque against the set, to which the camera shot, horizontally, through the cel's residual transparency. Thus houses and trees came in and out of view as the character walked along the street, and even the sky, mounted on rollers, was able to be moved. Absorbed as Cederquist was by two-dimensional representations of three-dimensional reality, Fleischer's strategy for handling parallax could not fail to make an impression on him. He set up a camera in front of the television set and began to take photographs of the cartoons, in part to give himself the sense that he was doing something constructive beyond being a good father by watching cartoons with his little girl. He then studied the "stills" to see how they worked (fig. 6), and from this came the idea to translate Olive's chair into wood, into *Olive's Chair*—a kind of three-dimensional drawing in constructed wood, the promotion to reality of an item in the logically flat cartoon world of Popeye, a bit like

Pygmalion turning a marble woman into flesh and blood, but also a bit different, since the statue and the woman displaced the same amount of space, whereas a drawing would have to be, so to speak, inflated. I cannot help but feel that there must have been some fantasy involved, a wish to occupy a world the artist could not enter, but parts of which he could bring into his own world. Popeye, like Cederquist, was a sailor man. In any case, a lot of the pieces in the show have the feeling of cartoon drawings. They look as if they were borrowed from one or another of the engine rooms on the boats Popeye sailed back and forth on, puffing steam. The *steam* could hardly be more cartoony.

Consider the remarkable headboard with the affecting title *When Machines Dream of Hokusai*. It consists of an effigy of a sort of still: two pipes, one coiled, the other serpentine, are connected to a spherical chamber (Pl. 43). The chamber is made of curved triangular plates, riveted together, just as the pipes consist of lengths riveted one to the other. A bit too much pressure has been built up in the chamber, as the puffs of steam clearly indicate, and as the pressure gauge, the needle of which points to an alarmingly high number, reveals. The still seems like a pretty primitive piece of machinery, supported by a rickety scaffolding of patched-together lumber, hardly to be counted on for much. But—and this is a miracle—out of the pipes' mouths gust marvelous dentellated waves of the sort we know from the famous print of Hokusai, *The Great Wave at Kanagawa*. The title of this piece confers a brilliance onto the work, which not merely unites the cartoon style of Popeye with the *ukiyo-e* style of the Japanese master, but does so in a way that is entirely Cederquist.

It is, of course, appropriate that a headboard should derive its iconography from the concept of a dream. (But how many headboards have exploited that opportunity?) Cederquist commented that a great many people have remarked on what they perceive as the sexual symbolism of waves gushing out of pipes, as if a nocturnal emission of spectacular proportion. If one insists upon being Freudian, there is perhaps a better theory available, namely, how repressed sexual energy becomes sublimated as art. But I was reminded of a brilliant conception of Saul Steinberg's, in which, for example, a patched-together cube is shown dreaming of itself as geometrically perfect, with sharp and numbered vertices, exact and lettered edges. I once commissioned Steinberg to design a poster for the fiftieth anniversary of the American Society for Aesthetics, of which I was president (fig. 7). We sent him some copies of our magazine, and he characteristically was fascinated by the typography, particularly the diphthong "Æ" in "Æsthetic." He drew us a plain E dreaming of being a diphthong, something really classy, a typographic promotion of which it could only dream, the way an anemic boy might dream of having perfect abs. The puff is cartoon for the dream, and Cederquist transforms dream puffs into dreamt waves. This is what a steampipe might dream about if it could dream. The equivalence between dream and art is made brilliantly visual, and at the same time perfectly autobiographical: Cederquist is a former surfer, whose inner life for the duration of this identity consisted of dreamt waves while his outer life consisted in chasing real ones. This, I think, explains his own identification with Hokusai.

AMERICAN SOCIETY FOR ÆSTHETICS
50TH ANNIVERSARY 1942-1992

fig. 7

fig. 8

fig. 9

In fact, the wave, as an emblem, intersects most of Cederquist's dimensions and enthusiasms. There is, to begin with, his history as a surfer, and from that period of his life he acquired an exact phenomenology of waves, as well as a special vocabulary which occasionally appears in the title of his works (e.g., *Tubular*). Then, of course, there is Popeye. The opening shot of every Popeye cartoon shows the bow of a ship surging through the waves, with the title of the cartoon on the forecastle doors with the Max Fleischer logo (fig. 8). And then there is Hokusai, whose great wave outranks the other wave images in the history of art by Courbet or Winslow Homer in terms of graphic feeling (fig. 5, p. 23). I was thrilled to discover that *The Great Wave* is quoted on the cover sheet of Popeye's theme song ("I'm Popeye the Sailor Man"), uniting two of Cederquist's inspirations in a single vivid image (fig. 9).

Cederquist is going through a Japanese phase, in which water and fish play central thematic roles, together with cunningly replicated scrap-wood structures, which have the air of disassembled packing crates given a second life. Needless to say, these often incorporate Japanese perspective, as if lifted from Japanese prints in the way that *Olive's Chair* was three-dimensionalized from its two-dimensional habitat in an animated cartoon. And the artist has gone so far as to inlay calligraphic inscriptions, which serve, for those who can read them, to express the work's intended spirit.

There is certainly nothing in the intarsia tradition that corresponds to the marvelous energy with which Cederquist's wave pieces are invested. The inlaid squirrel in the Urbino or the caged parrot in the Gubbio studiolo is pretty lifeless, and though there are waves in the classical repertoire of images upon which humanistic culture rested, as with Venus rising from the waves or Neptune being drawn in his fishy chariot through the waves by aquatic horses, the waves in those pictures are merely scenic effects and have no life of their own to contribute. The vision of nature Duke Federico contemplated was that of a mathematically ordered rational universe, whose emblems on his shelves were mathematical instruments. Even perspective served to demonstrate that the perceptual world, so standardly contrasted with true reality in the Platonist tradition, was itself mathematically organized. So nature is rarely if ever thought of as wild in Renaissance pictorial thought: one needs a different duke—Duke Ferdinand, in Shakespeare's *Tempest*—to be associated with waves like Hokusai's, and one has to wait for romanticism for that kind of blind surge and fierce indifference to human limitations, which Kant treated gingerly in his book on aesthetics, under the heading of the sublime. There are certainly high winds and storms at sea and in the Homeric epics. Still, these are caused by gods, like Neptune (Homer's Poseidon), who have it in for human beings and who control nature as a means of throwing their weight around. *The Great Wave* emblematizes an Oriental vision of pure natural force, as witness the fragile boats about to be swamped in Hokusai's print. And I suppose the surfer symbolizes a way in which a fragile human being on a gaudy platform can subdue wild nature by becoming one with it. In this sense, incorporating the wave in a piece of furniture carries forward the surfer's philosophy. *How to Wrap Five Waves*, then, executes the surfer's philosophy in the medium of wood: the waves are packed into wooden cases (Pl. 40).

The source for *How to Wrap Five Waves* is a text that had a certain cult status in the late 1960s called *How to Wrap Five Eggs*, a book about Japanese design. It belonged to the Zen subculture of that time, especially strong in Southern California, where Zen seemed to capture a certain idealized oneness with nature to which human beings might aspire through surfing, archery, or even motorcycle maintenance. Zen implies that nature has a certain "grain," and if we could discover it and so work with rather than against the grain, we could achieve wonders effortlessly. It was a very beautiful philosophy, and one I have felt the appeal of myself. Wrapping packages would have been a case in point, and *How to Wrap Five Eggs* shows the reader ways to wrap seemingly awkward objects—like five eggs—in beautiful ways.

To move from five eggs to five waves is sheer artistic creativity, suggested, I recently conjectured, by the possible play on the Spanish word for "eggs"—*huevos*—

which has the sound of "waves," allowing a neat interlingual pun. Cederquist is not fluent in Spanish, but California speech is filled with Spanish borrowings, the way New York ideolect is spiced with Yiddishisms, and at least one of his titles, *Cajón de los Muertos,* is in Spanish. Besides, he has a certain weakness for punning titles, like *Steamer Chest,* which is not at all a steamer chest in the exact meaning of the term but a pictorial composition of slats and a coiled pipe, emitting steam from both ends and through its seams (p. 4). One cannot get the full force of Cederquist's art if one is deaf to the humor. There is an inextricable cartoon streak in his mentality, as though he were constantly making offerings to the god of comedy. It is a rare attribute in an artist, for the entire spirit of the art world is on the side of dourness. If one looks for them, one can find jokes in Jesus' speech, but the Zen master routinely uses jokes to induce enlightenment. Not all of Cederquist's visual and verbal jokes are deep—but *How to Wrap Five Waves* is among those that are.

How to Wrap Five Waves is an inverted ziggurat, like the Guggenheim Museum, of stacked packing crates. It, like so many of Cederquist's pieces, is narrative. The ropes have been cut, the crates opened—one can see the removed slats at the top of the chest—and five great waves in graduated sizes are surging forward into the bedroom, serving, I suppose, as dream props for the occupant. They are definitely Japanese waves, and from the look of the crating and its inlaid inscriptions, the waves were packed in Japan. They fill the room with a stifled roar and the tacit salt smell of the crashing sea—what I suppose a surfer would wish to be able to package in order to be put in touch with the medium of his fulfillment. There can be very few pieces in the inventory of world art at once so funny and so poetic, so dense with the feeling of nature domesticated by craft and pictorial power, as improbable and as disciplined as this. It epitomizes a very rare artistic personality and a singular artistic achievement. It does for our time what the studioli did for the Renaissance.

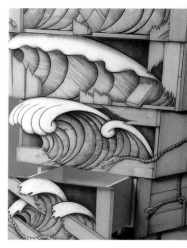

Detail, *How to Wrap Five Waves*

Fig. 1.   Studiolo of Federico da Montefeltro, duke of Urbino. Designer: Possibly Francesco di Giorgio of Siena. Intarsia: Workshop of Giuliano da Maiano. Provenance: Ducal Palace, Gubbio. General view. Walnut, spindle tree, oak, bog, mulberry, and fruit woods. The Metropolitan Museum of Art, Rogers Fund, 1939.

Fig. 2.   John Townsend, *High Chest,* ca. 1760. Mahogany, white pine, 87¼ x 39 x 20⅜ inches. Gift of Mr. and Mrs. Maxim Karolik Collection. Courtesy, Museum of Fine Arts, Boston.

Fig. 3.   John Cederquist, *Olive's Shoes.* Leather, fabric, crepe rubber, 4 x 6 x 9 inches.

Fig. 4.   Detail, Studiolo of Federico da Montefeltro, duke of Urbino. Bench with *mazzocchio.* Designer: Possibly Francesco di Giorgio of Siena. Intarsia: Workshop of Giuliano da Maiano. Provenance: Ducal Palace, Gubbio. Walnut, spindle tree, oak, bog, mulberry, and fruit woods. The Metropolitan Museum of Art, Rogers Fund, 1939.

Fig. 5.   Max Fleischer, diagram of setback. Courtesy Leslie Cabarga, *The Max Fleischer Story* (New York: Nostalgia Press, 1977).

Fig. 6.   Images from *Popeye* cartoons; photographed from a television screen. © 1997 King Features Syndicate, Inc. POPEYE and characters courtesy of King Features Syndicate, Inc. See Olive's chair in first frame.

Fig. 7.   Saul Steinberg, poster for the American Society for Aesthetics. Permission American Society for Aesthetics and Saul Steinberg.

Fig. 8.   *Popeye* cartoon title; photographed from a television screen. © 1997 King Features Syndicate, Inc. POPEYE and characters courtesy of King Features Syndicate, Inc.

Fig. 9.   Cover, Popeye's theme song ("I'm Popeye the Sailor Man"). Popeye image copyright King Features Syndicate. Courtesy Leslie Cabarga, *The Max Fleischer Story* (New York: Nostalgia Press, 1977).

john cederquist: theater in the round

Nancy Princenthal

It is customary, and from some points of view necessary, to make a distinction between fine art and useful or technological art. But the point of view from which it is necessary is one that is extrinsic to the work of art itself.
— John Dewey[1]

There are lots of junctures in the course of modernism where art and furniture cross lines. Brancusi, Noguchi, Judd, and Siah Armajani (fig. 1)—the last a great admirer of Dewey, who is quoted in Armajani's work—are just a random handful of the many artists to have jumped tracks conspicuously and often. But these moves have all taken place on the field of sculpture. To execute them on the picture plane is to change the rules entirely—it is, as John Cederquist has done, to press one's nose right up against Alice's looking glass.

Beyond that glass is a theatrical world which, like Carroll's, is rich with conventions elaborated until they twist. But if Cederquist's career is built on images that (again, like Carroll's) address the mind's eye independently of the body's, his furniture is also as American as Dewey in its utility, its shamelessly broad appeal (call it populism), and, not least, its altogether earthbound sense of humor.

physical comedy

In the early 1980s Cederquist began making furniture whose surfaces and shapes bear pictorial information that is at variance, obliquely, with their physical reality. Photographed from the right place, *Olive's Chair* (Pl. 4; it was inspired by furniture in an old Popeye cartoon) looks unremarkable—nearly unnoticeable, in fact, in its ordinariness. Even its dimensions (38 x 18 x 14 in.) don't give it away. But it can't be used. Its seat tips down and is a narrow, irregular diamond, not a rectangle; its legs are uneven; it would spill any sitter as surely as any vaudevillian's banana peel. The slightly later *Three Folding Chairs* (1982–83) are even less accommodating: the

fig. 1

impression that they are fully volumetric only holds from a single vantage point (the one from which they are generally photographed). These chairs, along with *2-D Thonet* (Pl. 12), a svelte, elegant, and equally dysfunctional side chair, were all copied from a 1904 catalogue of Michael Thonet's bentwood furniture. From the same catalogue came a 1982 *Game Table* (Pl. 2)—with Cederquist, all double entendres are intended—the top of which is raised to show a board for chess on one side and for backgammon on the other, neither one available for use.

Some words are closely enough related to form neatly paradoxical oppositions: *illusion/deception* is one such pair that has particular relevance to Cederquist's undertaking. The first term rests securely within the protocols of art (and polite society); the second belongs just as decisively outside its margins. The difference between them rests on the complicity that can be assumed with the agent of the effect. To entertain an illusion, to give it credence, is to share in a communicable understanding (this distinguishes it also from a delusion); it is to recognize a shared language, spoken with particular fluency. A deception can be pulled off in such a way that it inspires respect for skill and wit (this separates it from flat-out deceit), but it is not extended in the spirit of open communication. Deception is meant to conceal something from the viewer, whereas illusion generally makes things exceptionally plain.

That illusion belongs to pictorial representation while deception belongs to, say, card tricks, and that neither really belongs in the world of solid objects is just the kind of rock-solid convention that piques Cederquist's fancy—as it does a very few other artists: Bruce Nauman comes to mind. Making much of his work in the interface between visual and verbal puns, Nauman does not shy from big questions impertinently phrased. One concerns the exchanges between art and artful dodgery. In a five-panel video installation of 1993 called *Falls, Pratfalls, and Sleights of Hand* (fig. 2), Nauman presented, in wall-sized enlargement and relentless slow motion, the hapless grace of trained actors taking falls, as chairs literally slipped from under them. The humor, the faint trace of cruelty, and above all the mesmerizing credibility of these exercises—despite the slowed-down action, it is virtually impossible to spot the moment when the fall is staged—have a lot to do with Cederquist's elegant, unaccommodating early furniture pieces and the utterly convincing lies they tell. Despite their self-sufficiency, they are easily imagined as props in a slapstick routine, the kind where the humor of the gestures depends on the consummate dignity of the players.

character development

Though the impossible table and chairs were as intellectually bountiful as they were physically inhospitable, Cederquist soon began to search for forms that had, as it were, more of a shelf life. It is telling that, though trained as a craftsman,[2] he made illusionistic functional furniture only after this conceptual detour. An extended series of chests of drawers was begun in the late 1980s. Their basic configuration and decorative schemes were determined by illustrational conventions borrowed from a range of popular sources—cartoons, primarily, and even such Pop-derived, painterly realism as Wayne Thiebaud's vibrant still lifes, but also more generalized forms of cultural shorthand. While Cederquist's chests of drawers actually work as such, illusionism still prevails: many of the applied pictorial clues, including receding contours and shadows, conceal the actual shape and size of the furniture.

Auntie Macassar Goes West (Pl. 7), perhaps the most explicitly figurative of these pieces, is a five-drawer chest inlaid with a flowery mauve Formica in front; the drawers' protruding sides are, rather indecorously, left au naturel. The top drawer, finished in barefaced pale purple Formica, seems to be, untidily, a little open, even when closed. This illusion is created by Cederquist's having made a shadow below it of a darker shade of formica and by "exposing" part of the side of the drawer, fake dovetail joints and all, in a drawing executed in epoxy laid into routed grooves. On top of the chest, a couple of concealed toiletries seem to prop up a gold-colored scarf (or, antimacassar), which drapes, carelessly, over the top drawer as well. All slopes down, as if corseted, to dainty little legs.

2-D Thonet

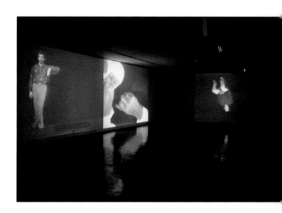

fig. 2

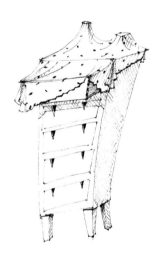

Auntie Macassar Goes West, drawing

Detail, *Cleo*

As convincingly drawn a character study as she is a piece of furniture, *Auntie Macassar* was followed by a suite of equally colorful individuals. *Cleo* (Pl. 18), though named for a character in the movie *Pinocchio,* could as easily be the doting Auntie's favorite niece. Here, a simpler, red-bordered square of *faux* linen is thrown across the chest's top and highest drawer, which is again made to look as if it was left carelessly ajar, though in reality all is flat as the facade of a boomtown saloon. The skin of this dresser is an innocent shade of pale poplar, and the "handles" are faced in gray Formica. (As is often the case with Cederquist, the hardware of these drawer pulls involves a delightfully simple trick. Though fake shadows suggest they protrude, they are actually flush. To use them, you push in one spring-loaded corner and pull from the inside.) On top, in a final flourish of illusion, a pretend goldfish (Cleo, in the Pinocchio story) inhabits a make-believe bowl.

Spicing up this furniture family's life is the irrepressible *Mexican Madness* (Pl. 14), a Carmen Miranda of a dresser in which sprightly gray drawers alternate with flouncy red ruffles. The round mirror on top seems set at an angle jaunty as a fruit-trimmed hat, though it is actually flush with the chest's front surface.

putting It on the road

As hard as they push against traditional expectations for functional form (and for sculpture, and for graphic art), these three chests all begin with some kind of furniture imagery. The way they polarize image and reality is by materializing both, but on different planes. In most subsequent chests of drawers, Cederquist mixes it up even more, moving from paradox to flagrant metaphor. It is a move that clearly distinguishes his work from the Pop-based sculpture/furniture of, say, Richard Artschwager or Claes Oldenburg (fig. 3), whose main rhetorical device is irony. The ways in which chests support transience, and concealment—the way they model a break between content and form, since what's outside doesn't tell you anything about what's inside—find expression (and always at least one good joke) in such works as *Le Fleuron Manquant, Kimono-to-Go, Tubular,* and *Little Wave.* In these pieces, Cederquist's imagery grows more complex, and its sources more diverse.

In 1989 Cederquist was invited to participate in an exhibition of new furniture commissioned to reinterpret objects from the collection of the Museum of Fine

fig. 3

Arts, Boston. Cederquist's response was to repackage, rather literally, a celebrated eighteenth-century highboy by John Townsend. With a wary eye turned toward deconstructionist theory, then all the rage in architecture, Cederquist created *Le Fleuron Manquant (The Missing Finial)* (Pl. 13). It is a helter-skelter arrangement of trompe-l'oeil crates, each containing, in two-dimensional effigy, a disassembled piece of Townsend's chest (except, of course, the notoriously misplaced finial). Reducing Townsend's sacred icon to a series of disconnected fragments, and fitting them together with all the serendipity of Kurt Schwitters's *Merzbau* (fig. 4), Cederquist fashioned a thoroughly secular reliquary, to which pieties of religion and theory are equally alien.

fig. 4

Though born in happenstance, the vocabulary of furniture-as-packing-crate has proved remarkably durable for Cederquist. *Kimono-to-Go* (Pl. 19) develops it, while articulating a connection, always at least implicit in his work, to Japanese art and craft. If *Le Fleuron Manquant* mimed American-abroad cultural clumsiness, *Kimono-to-Go* is a study in visual agility. Drawing on origami as well as Japanese apparel, it (seemingly) causes deftly folded patterned silk to (seem to) emerge from an upended wooden crate, precariously perched on (seeming) bits of scrap wood. Clearly, Cederquist is attracted to those traditional forms of folding, whether of paper or cloth, by which three-dimensional form emerges, rather magically, from flat materials.

Tubular (Pl. 17), like the slightly less elaborate *Little Wave* (Pl. 20), points to another, even more important connection in Cederquist's work with the art of Japan, which is through woodblock prints. Rendering illusionistic scenes on two-dimensional wood surfaces is a skill that reached its height in the *ukiyo-e* woodblock prints of the eighteenth and nineteenth centuries, prints that celebrate the richly symbolic realm of the "floating world" (again, the connection to Cederquist's work is apparent). Some of the contours in Cederquist's imagery are actually incised, as in intaglio prints (though Cederquist fills the routed lines with dark-colored epoxy, so they read as positives, whereas the incised lines of woodblock prints read as negatives). More to the point, Cederquist lifts images intact from favorite *ukiyo-e* masters, the crashing, foam-capped waves in Hokusai's *Thirty-six Views of Fuji* (fig. 5) in particular. In *Tubular* (the reference to the perfect wave comes legitimately to Cederquist, a Californian and an avid surfer), a curving wall of water surges up through a stack of crates, spilling (so to speak) over the top. The stacked ersatz boxes, some inscribed with Japanese characters,[3] are depicted as mostly broken by the force of the wave, which culminates in a stylized lather of sea spray.

Detail, *Tubular*

In both of these chests, something with the imperative of a full-scale typhoon is clearly being shipped from East to West, and though it may not survive the passage intact, its influence can't be denied. What's more, the effort to break it up and repackage it has been largely unavailing. Although fewer Americans can name Hokusai than Japanese can name Walt Disney (or Krazy Kat, or Sinbad the Sailor, to name some cartoon characters that Cederquist admires), this wave, as image and metaphor, is a nearly universal symbol.

fig. 5

But *Tubular* is more than a rousing testament to the vicissitudes of cultural exchange. It is also a remarkably ingenious piece of craftsmanship, in which Cederquist's illusionism has progressed to the point where it becomes nearly impossible to mentally reconstruct the relationship between actual and depicted volumes, even after a physical demonstration. For instance, the front is no longer a flat facade. Instead, the sides of the crates slope away from their leading faces, but at a wider angle than the drawers they harbor, while devilishly varied arrangements have been made for opening their false fronts. In the movies, these would be called special effects: optical and physical tricks in which, *Roger Rabbit*–style, the stuntmen are one dimension short of reality. Of course, a sleight of hand should not be mistaken for a short cut; having pictorial body-doubles, in furniture, means twice the work. And the skillful effort is itself part of the picture. Just as Cederquist establishes a connection between Hokusai and Hollywood, so he recalibrates Pop art's high/low equation by entering fine craft into the balance. It is a factor that generally counts for more in popular culture but, turned against itself—as, say, in *Tubular*—noticeably shifts its weight.

Deconstructionist
Saw Chair

Detail,
Untitled (Saw Chair)

seating plans

In the early 1990s Cederquist turned again to seating, this time functional. Chairs have a much stronger record of survival in the free-fire zone between art and craft than highboys or gaming tables. Though all furniture can be called anthropocentric to the degree that it responds to human bodily needs, chairs are most nearly figurative; they not only support the body closely but also (having arms, legs, and backs) resemble it. What's more, they breed several varieties of transcendence, from humble elevation above physical discomfort to more ambitious flights of fancy. Elaine Scarry has written that the satisfaction of physical needs involves making the world act as if it were sentient—it requires imbuing inanimate things with characteristics of compassion. Moreover, Scarry says, that process allows for—indeed suggests the image of—things less immediately necessary. For instance, "The human being, troubled by weight, creates a chair; the chair recreates him to be weightless; and now he projects this new weightless self into new objects, the image of an angel, the design for a flying machine."4

Scarry is altogether serious about the causal relationship between tool making and spiritual excursions. Though they intend no cynicism, Cederquist's chairs and sofas stage take-offs that are decidedly irreverent; sometimes, for instance, they seem to levitate on little Looney-Tune puffs of steam. (His references to the floating world of premodern Japan are no more pious.) Even in those chairs visibly rooted to the ground, form and function—or, pictorial imagination and its bodily seat—are pulled apart altogether unceremoniously. While such divisions occur throughout Cederquist's work, they have lately evolved from polite opposition to a bit of a barroom brawl. Hence *Deconstructionist Saw Chair* (Pl. 28) and *Untitled (Saw Chair)* (Pl. 33), both 1993, in which murderous circular saw blades (drawn as ellipses, as if in perspectival rendering) dominate the narrow backs of all-too-vulnerable-looking assemblages of misaligned boards. Apart from physical ease and its opposite, there are other renunciations at play in this work. One target is the venerable modernist maxim that good design exalts the inherent qualities of materials and the fabrication process; another target, of course, is a still prestigious brand of cultural theory.

Similarly, Cederquist sets up the idea that design should be "organic," that is, should harmonize with natural patterns of generation and growth, in *Worms Go In, Worms Go Out* (Pl. 34). This parody of self-consumption takes the form of a double-wide seat in which colossal green worms crawl around a ramshackle construction of *faux* two by fours. In other work, wood is made to coexist with its archrival, steam, and also great tides of salt water. *Couchabunga* (Pl. 27) reprises the theme of *Tubular* and *Little Wave*, this time with a fairly tame wave curving over part of the seat back, in a couch that looks well on its way to being sea wrack. *Steaming Poodle Bench* (Pl. 37), part of a new, cartoon-influenced series, joins coils of bursting pipes (all still actually made of wood) with what seem precariously rigged seats and legs. Escaping jets of painted steam—their puffy termini suggest clipped poodle legs—not only lift the pipes off the floor, they also mark the armrest's end, suggesting less than calming repose.

But it is in the pictorial program of the *Marquis de Side Chairs I* (Pl. 24) and *II* (Pl. 30) that visible comfort is most obviously confounded. The first is a mock fauteuil, the second a narrower and more straitened affair, without arms. In both, vaguely erotic rococo decorative devices—stylized scrolls that could be commas, too, or quotation marks, but are also vaguely phallic—are combined, willy-nilly, with the odd instrument of abuse (principally a nail-studded ball, itself not devoid of sexual overtones). What began, at the outset of Cederquist's career, as a fairly abstract expression of unease—the mismatch between image and physical fact—has come round, in these chairs, to a depiction of physical pain as unremitting, and ultimately harmless, as a half hour with Tom and Jerry.

integrity and its double

While chairs have historically appealed to sculptors more than other furniture forms (not least because they're a good deal easier to engineer than, say, a chest of drawers), they pose distinctive challenges to the art-minded. For one thing, they can't easily be looked at and used at the same time. More to the point for Cederquist, they have neither a continuous front on which to execute illusionistic imagery nor unseen, inner compartments against which to set, in conceptual counterpoint, other forms of concealment and deception.

Still, as expression, furniture all tends to cluster around a position on the truth/falsehood spectrum that is distinctly different from, say, photorealism. It can, without too much strain, be called an ethical position, since the question isn't just whether furniture is more decidably verifiable, by use, than painting. Furniture, unlike painting (or sculpture) can also be good—can help out, materially—in a way that pictures can't. This is not exactly what Scott Burton had in mind when he described his work, which crossed over from sculpture to public furniture (fig. 6) as "a rebuke to the art world,"[5] but it's close. "No mere maker of visual signs can be exemplary, can propose a sufficient moral authority or model of psychic liberation in a time like ours," Burton said in 1980. To replace these mere sign makers, Burton heralded "a new visual culture of design or applied art," in which "content is more than the private history of its maker."[6]

Sounding resoundingly utopian and distinctly Bauhausian (though he was always also both funny and subversive), Burton also spoke for his moment in articulating an impatience bordering on contempt for the arts of self-expression, which, in the form of Italian and German neoexpressionist painting, were then enjoying a fairly frenzied success. Burton, Siah Armajani, and the artists of their generation who became involved with designs for public seating (and lighting, landscaping, pedestrian traffic, etc.) generally considered their undertaking a way to make art less autocratic and more responsive to a range of issues that ran from social and historical to physical. But public furniture is not the only way to realize these goals; turning the mass media against themselves and mobilizing various communities to help generate public art are just two alternatives.

Cederquist's work falls into this history from a position of quite unchallenged solitude. Clearly, he engages the legacy of painterly realism, with all the authorial prerogative it speaks for, but he is not a realist painter. Just as obviously he partakes of the legacy of Pop art and subsequent art-world jousts with the mass media, especially syndicated cartoon strips and commercial animation. Roy Lichtenstein belongs

fig. 6

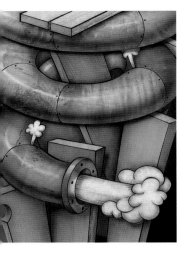

Detail, *Steamer Chest III*

among his sources, for giving independent physical presence to pictorial representation's constituent parts—brushstrokes, Benday dots (fig. 7)—and so does René Magritte, for separating, but only by inches, reality from realism .

But Cederquist is neither a Pop artist nor a surrealist, and he doesn't make furniture as an ethical choice. He makes it, clearly, for pleasure and often for laughter, in pursuit of which he doesn't scorn cornball jokes. *Steamer Chest III* (Pl. 41), a companion to the *Steaming Poodle Bench* (Pl. 37), is a coiled, conical tower of (seeming) pipes filled to bursting, set against a rickety scaffold of broken boards. It is a funny image, even a silly one, and for all its references to outmoded conveyances and their appointments (steamships, clunky, leather-strapped chests) and to outmoded industries (steam-powered manufacturing, handmade furniture), it is also an exuberant image, fairly bubbling over with manic energy. Though *Cajón de los Muertos* (Pl. 39), another recent chest of drawers, is nominally morbid, it has an equally high-spirited kind of ghoulishness, its exposed skull and picturesquely broken boards suggesting piratical misdeeds on the high seas, and just desserts for the miscreants, in fictionally tidy proportions.

How to Wrap Five Waves (Pl. 40) is a precarious-looking chest of progressively larger drawers, the smallest at the bottom, each holding a surging wave, unavailingly. Here, the joke is on a well-respected Japanese design text about devising ways to wrap five eggs. But if wrapping eggs is a challenge that elicits working principles of profound importance to design, wrapping waves (whether of water or stylistic influence) is a problem that has no material resolution, however productive it is for abstract thought.

There is no solution because there is no problem, Duchamp famously said of art, in an epigram that seems to distinguish the "fine from the useful arts." It is Cederquist's achievement to bring the same degree of cheerful superfluousness—of anarchy, illusion, and frank excess—to objects generally placed among the realm of practical solutions. There is, in design, no higher value than "integrity," taken to mean economical responses to definable practical needs, and open expression of form. It is in a way Cederquist's central motivation to simply invert this program, so that deception replaces candor as a working principle. Gullibility and belief, magic and imaginative transcendence, are shuffled in his work, too deftly for us to be sure of what we see. *Stroke of Genius* (Pl. 35), a 1994 chair is called. A housepainter's brush, still loaded, hangs upright over the seat it's just conjured into existence. Hardly a single detail of this object can be called functionally necessary, or visually reliable, but it works like a charm.

fig. 7

Notes

1. John Dewey, *Art as Experience* (New York: G. P. Putnam, 1980), p. 26.

2. Cederquist graduated from Long Beach State (now California State University, Long Beach) with a B.A. in art and an M.A. in crafts. His early work, influenced by Wendell Castle, was sculptural but functional, and included molded-leather elements. He also made Art Nouveau–inspired bentwood chairs and rockers.

3. One translates as "hollow wave," the other is Hokusai's cartouche.

4. Elaine Scarry, *The Body in Pain: The Making and Unmaking of the World* (New York and Oxford: Oxford University Press, 1985), p. 321.

5. Scott Burton, conversation with the author, spring 1987.

6. Quoted in "Situation Aesthetics: Impermanent Art and the Seventies Audience," *Artforum* 18 (January 1980): 23.

Fig. 1. Siah Armajani. *Meeting Garden*, 1980. Painted wood, corrugated steel, Plexiglas. Artpark, Lewiston, New York. Photograph courtesy Max Protetch Gallery, New York.

Fig. 2. Bruce Nauman. *Falls, Pratfalls, and Sleights of Hand*, 1993. Five-panel video installation. © 1997 Bruce Nauman/Artists Rights Society (ARS), New York.

Fig. 3. Claes Oldenburg. *Bedroom Ensemble*, 1963. Wood, vinyl, metal, artificial fur, cloth, and paper. Courtesy National Gallery of Canada, Ottawa.

Fig. 4. Kurt Schwitters, *Der Merzbau*, Hannover, 1933. Courtesy Sprengel Museum, Hannover. © 1997 Artists Rights Society (ARS), New York/VG Bild-Kunst, Bonn.

Fig. 5. Katsushika Hokusai. From *The Thirty-six Views of Fuji* (1823–29). *The Great Wave at Kanagawa*. Woodcut, $9\frac{7}{8}$ x $14\frac{7}{8}$ inches. The Metropolitan Museum of Art, Henry L. Phillips Collection, Bequest of Henry L. Phillips, 1939 (JP 2972).

Fig. 6. Scott Burton. Equitable Center, New York City, South Plaza, 1986. Granite. Photograph courtesy Max Protetch Gallery, New York.

Fig. 7. Roy Lichtenstein, *Little Big Painting*, 1965. Oil and synthetic polymer on canvas. 68 x 80 inches. Purchase, with funds from the Friends of the Whitney Museum of American Art, New York (66.2). Photograph Copyright © 1996: Whitney Museum of American Art, New York. Photograph by Geoffrey Clements, New York.

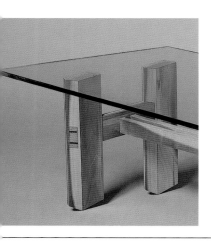

1. first piece, 1981

Glass, Baltic birch plywood, poplar,
embuia inlay
Wood frame, 16 x 25 x 14 inches;
glass top, 44 x 19 inches
John Cederquist

2. game table, 1982

Baltic birch plywood, maple,
purpleheart inlay, aniline dye, metal hardware
48 x 32 x 21 inches
Lent by Gloria and Sonny Kamm,
Encino, California

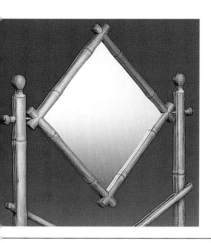

3. jungle dresser, 1982
Baltic birch plywood, pecan, East Indian
rosewood inlay, mirror, glass, pencil, dye
59 x 38 x 14 inches
Collection of Warren Rubin and Bernice
Wollman, Bayonne, New Jersey

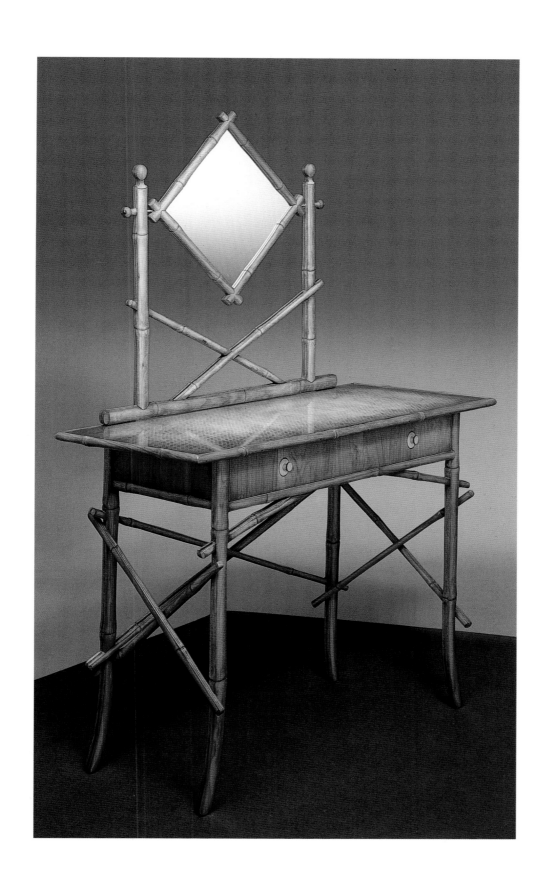

4. olive's chair, 1982
Baltic birch plywood, Spanish cedar,
embuia inlay, leather, aniline dye
38 x 18 x 14 inches
Lent by Mr. and Mrs. Smith

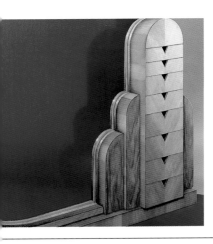

5. art deco mirror, 1983
Baltic birch plywood, Sitka spruce,
Andaman Island padauk, East Indian
rosewood inlay, mirror, aniline dye
70 x 67 x 12 inches
Photograph courtesy John Cederquist

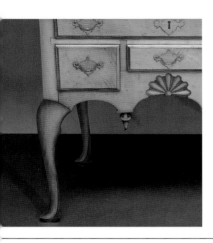

6. lowboy, 1983

Baltic birch plywood, maple, koa,
East Indian rosewood inlay,
aniline dye, paint
30 x 34 x 16 inches
John Cederquist

7. auntie macasser goes west, 1984

Baltic birch plywood, nutmeg, poplar,
Colorcore Formica, epoxy resin inlay, aniline dye
64 x 38 x 12 inches
Collection of the Oakland Museum of California,
gift of the Collectors Gallery, the Art Guild,
Anne and Ronald Abramson, the Timken Fund,
Virginia and Andy Lewis, Shelby and Frederick Gans,
and Sandra G. and Steven Wolfe

8. the great art deco furniture explosion, 1984

Baltic birch plywood, bird's-eye maple, Colorcore
Formica, purpleheart inlay, aniline dye
69 x 40 x 14 inches
Collection of Warren Rubin and Bernice Wollman,
Bayonne, New Jersey

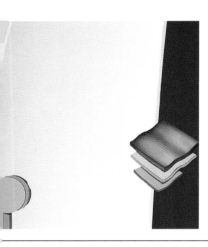

9. blade mirror, 1985
Baltic birch plywood, Sitka spruce,
Colorcore Formica, epoxy resin inlay,
aniline dye, mirror
55 x 15 x 5 inches
Photograph courtesy John Cederquist

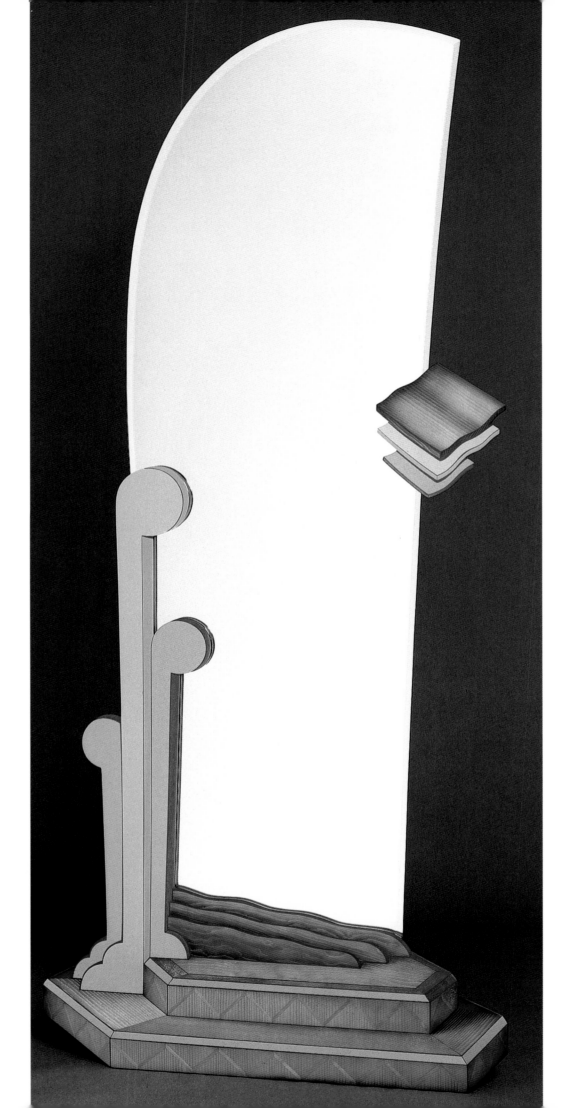

10. designer crates, 1985

Baltic birch plywood, Sitka spruce,
embuia inlay, aniline dye
69¼ x 39½ x 12⅞ inches
Lent by Anne and Ronald Abramson

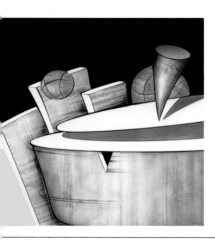

11. top drawer, 1985
Baltic birch plywood, Sitka spruce, maple,
Colorcore Formica, epoxy resin inlay,
aniline dye, metal hardware
70 x 38¼ x 15 inches
Lent by Anne and Ronald Abramson

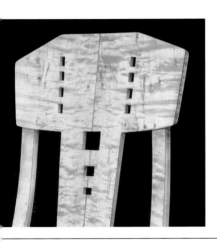

12. 2-d thonet, 1985

Baltic birch plywood, maple,
embuia inlay, aniline dye
39 x 25½ x 13 inches
Courtesy The Art Institute of Chicago,
Gift of Darlene V. Shane and
Lawrence Caplan, M.D.

13. le fleuron manquant (the missing finial), 1989

Baltic birch plywood, mahogany, koa,
Sitka spruce, purpleheart inlay, epoxy
resin inlay, metal hardware, aniline dye
78⅝ x 35 x 12½ inches
Lent courtesy of a private collection, Boston

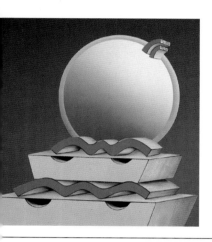

14. mexican madness, 1989

Baltic birch plywood, Sitka spruce,
Colorcore Formica, epoxy resin inlay, mirror,
aniline dye, metal hardware
72 x 40 x 14 inches
Lent by Charles and Mapes Stamm

15. deco world, 1990

Baltic birch plywood, maple,
Colorcore Formica, mirror
72 x 29 x 6 inches
Collection of Janet and Robert Cardon,
New York

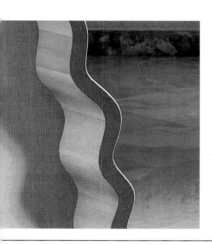

16. mr. wiggle, 1990
Baltic birch plywood, Sitka spruce,
Colorcore Formica, epoxy resin inlay,
aniline dye, mirror
72 x 36 x 5 inches
Collection American Craft Museum,
New York, Gift of Tera Cederquist, 1991

17. tubular, 1990

Baltic birch plywood, Sitka spruce,
maple, epoxy resin inlay, aniline dye,
oil-based lithography inks, metal hardware
84 x 48 x 16 inches
Lent by Robert and Gayle Greenhill,
Greenwich, Connecticut

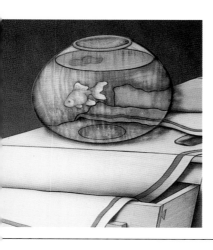

18. cleo, 1990–91

Baltic birch plywood, poplar, maple,
nutmeg, Colorcore Formica, oil-based
lithography inks, metal hardware
65 x 40 x 15 inches
Collection of Franklin and Suzi Parrasch,
New York

19. kimono-to-go, 1990–91

Baltic birch plywood, maple,
Sitka spruce, gold leaf, epoxy resin inlay,
aniline dye, metal hardware
78 x 36 x 14½ inches
Lent by the MCI World Headquarters,
Washington, D.C.

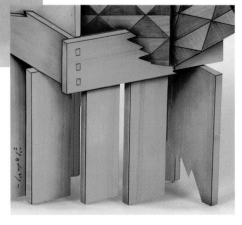

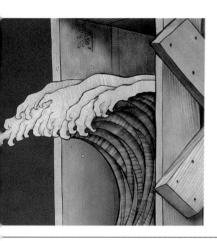

20. little wave, 1990–91

Baltic birch plywood, Sitka spruce,
maple, epoxy resin inlay, aniline dye,
metal hardware, oil-based lithography inks
78 x 38 x 15 inches
Lent courtesy of the Ann and Jerry Milne Collection,
Washington, D.C.

21. gumby's first attempt at zen, 1991

Baltic birch plywood, Sitka spruce, Colorcore Formica,
epoxy resin inlay, aniline dye, mirror
81 x 28 x 23 inches
Mitchell Berliner Collection

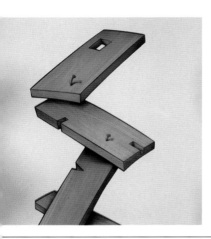

22. rietveldt's first attempt at the zig-zag chair, 1991

Baltic birch plywood, poplar,
epoxy resin inlay, aniline dye
48 x 18 x 20 inches
Lent by Mr. and Mrs. Peter R. Coneway, Houston

23. wannabe, 1991

Baltic birch plywood, Sitka spruce,
embuia inlay, epoxy resin inlay,
aniline dye, metal hardware
86 x 40 x 20 inches
Lent courtesy of
Mitchell Berliner Collection

24. marquis de side chair I, 1991-92

Baltic birch plywood, poplar, Sitka spruce, maple,
nutmeg, epoxy resin inlay, aniline dye
32 x 32 x 29 inches
Lent by Judie and Howard Ganek,
New York

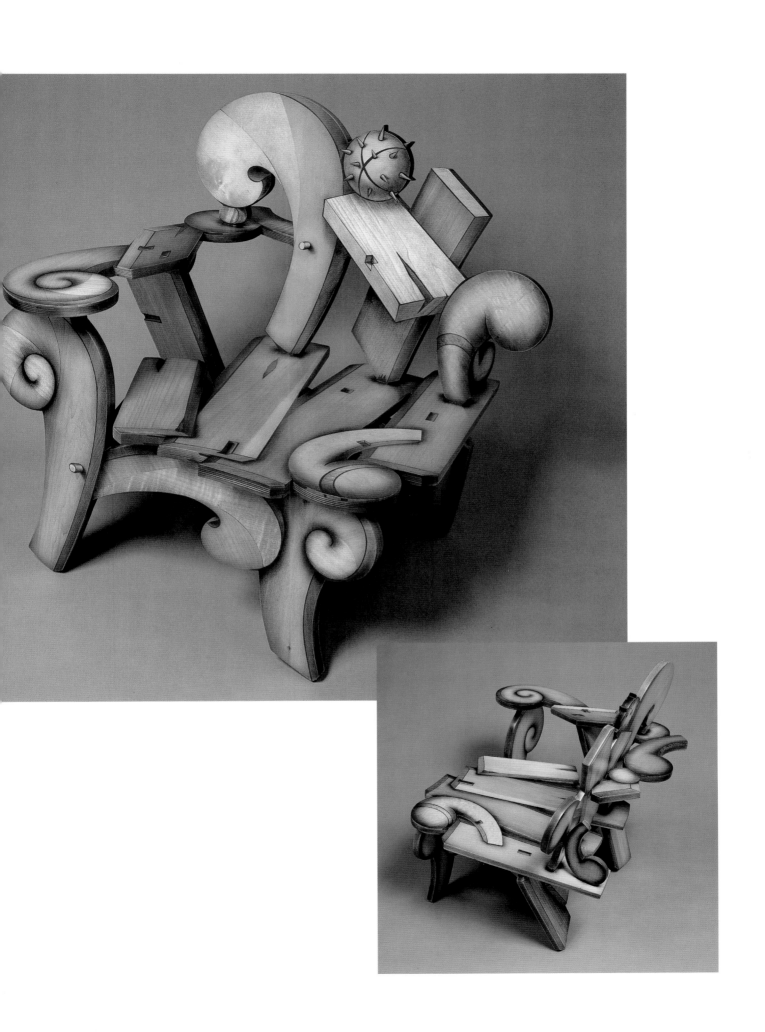

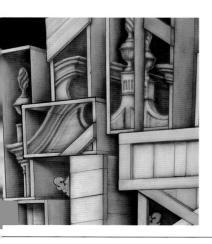

25. ghost boy, 1992

Baltic birch plywood, Sitka spruce,
poplar, copper leaf, epoxy resin inlay,
aniline dye, paint, metal hardware
88¼ x 44½ x 15 inches
National Museum of American Art,
Smithsonian Institution,
Gift of the James Renwick Alliance,
Ronald and Anne Abramson,
and museum purchase

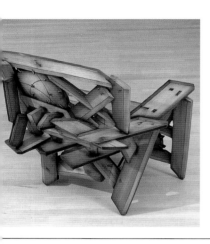

26. the three attempts of marquis de side, 1992

Baltic birch plywood, poplar, nutmeg,
maple, epoxy resin inlay, aniline dye
28 x 33 x 25 inches
Lent courtesy of the Peter T. Joseph Collection

27. couchabunga, 1992–93
Baltic birch plywood, basswood, maple,epoxy resin inlay, oil-based lithography inks, aniline dye
29 x 60 x 25 inches
Lent by Daphne Farago Collection, Little Compton, Rhode Island

28. deconstructionist saw chair, 1993

Baltic birch plywood, Sitka spruce, maple,
epoxy resin inlay, aniline dye
49 x 17 x 26 inches
Lent by John W. and Marilyn L. Barrett,
Bethesda, Maryland

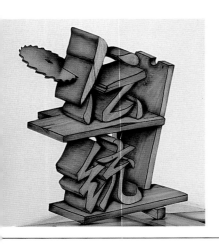

29. dento, 1993

Baltic birch plywood,
maple, epoxy resin inlay, aniline dye
41 x 42 x 36 inches
Lent courtesy of Mitchell Berliner Collection

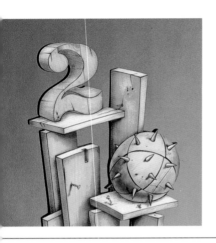

30. marquis de side chair II, 1993

Baltic birch plywood, poplar, maple,
nutmeg, epoxy resin inlay, aniline dye
60 x 20 x 26 inches
Collection of Miles and Lyn Lourie,
Coconut Grove, Florida

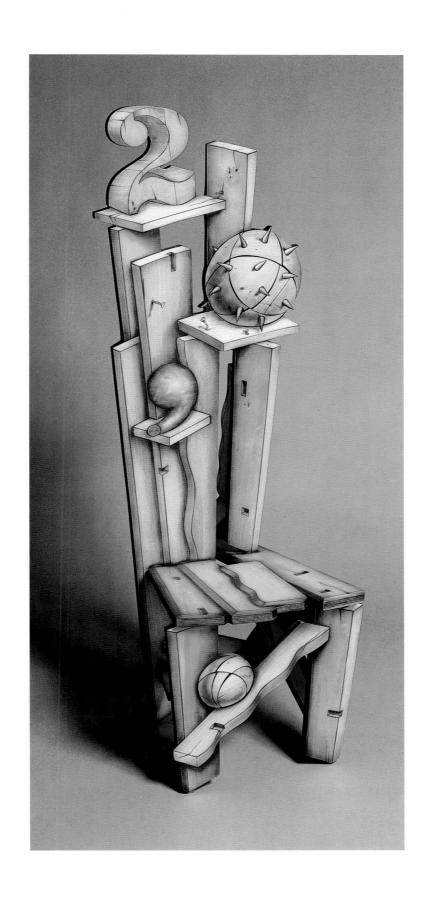

31. revenge of the deconstructionist saw chair, 1993

Baltic birch plywood, Sitka spruce, maple,
epoxy resin inlay, aniline dye
51 x 17 x 26 inches
Yale University Art Gallery, Please Be Seated
Collection, funded by Julian H. Fisher, B.A. 1969,
in Memory of Wilbur J. Fisher, B.A. 1926, and
Janet H. Fisher

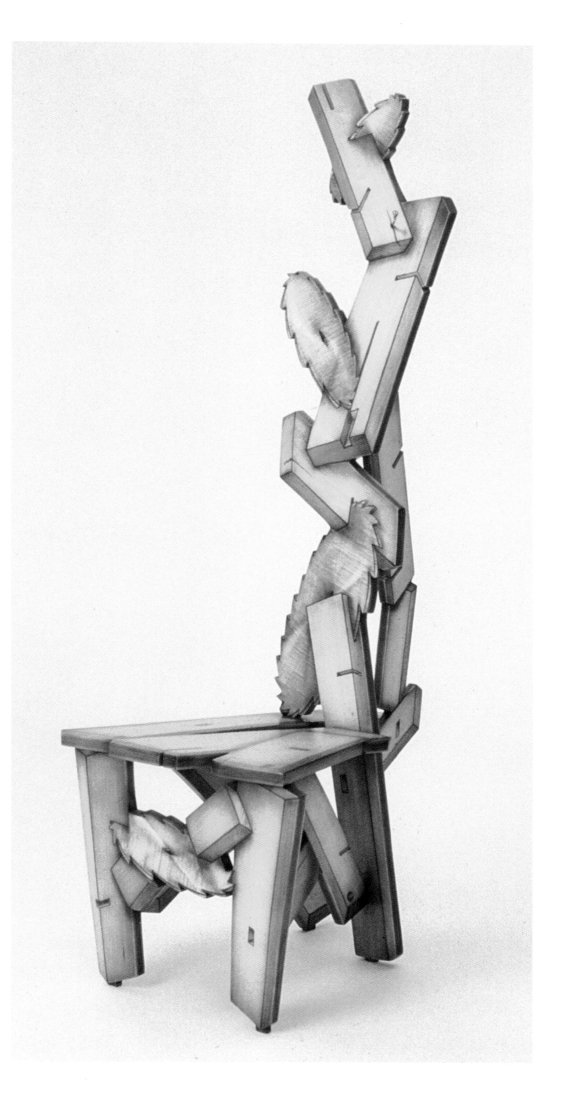

32. tsunami tsidechair, 1993

Baltic birch plywood, poplar, maple,
epoxy resin inlay, oil-based lithography inks, aniline dye
33 x 28 x 25 inches
Lent by Arlene and Harvey Caplan,
Short Hills, New Jersey

33. untitled
(saw chair), 1993

Baltic birch plywood, poplar, maple,
epoxy resin inlay, aniline dye
37 x 19 x 24 inches
Lent by Robert and Gayle Greenhill,
Greenwich, Connecticut

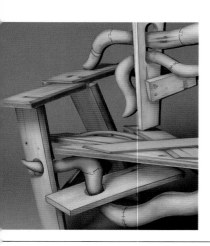

34. worms go in, worms go out, 1993

Baltic birch plywood, poplar,
maple, epoxy resin inlay, aniline dye
31 x 60 x 24 inches
Lent by Charles and Mapes Stamm

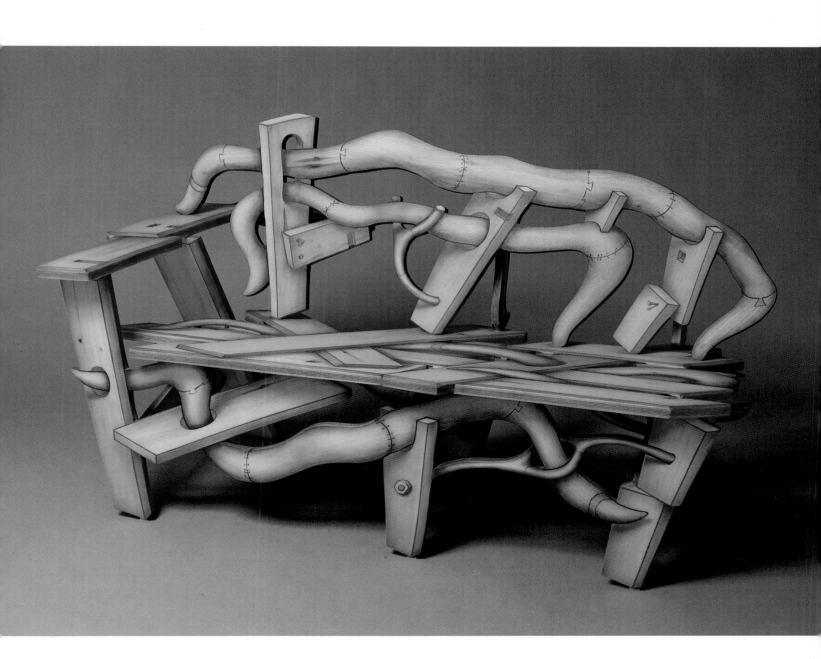

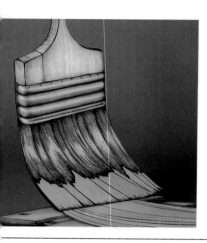

35. stroke of genius, 1994

Baltic birch plywood, basswood, alder, poplar, maple,
epoxy resin inlay, oil-based lithography inks, aniline dye
46 x 36 x 30 inches
Lent courtesy of the Carolyn J. and
Robert C. Springborn Collection

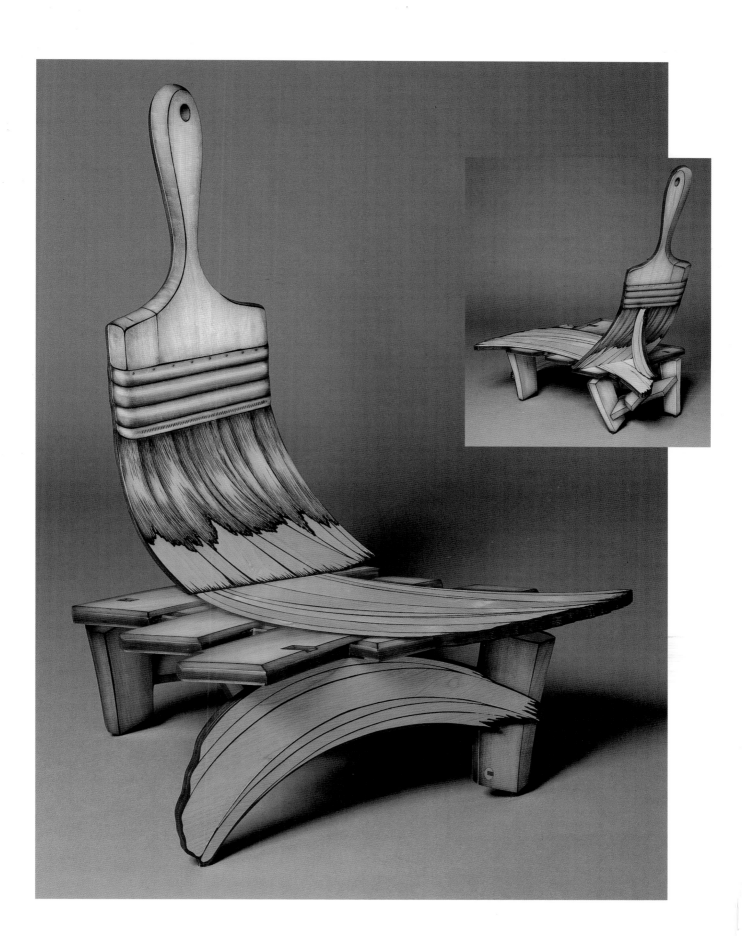

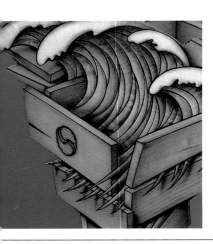

36. tsunami under glass, 1994

Glass, Baltic birch plywood, Sitka spruce,
maple, epoxy resin inlay,
oil-based lithography inks, aniline dye
36 x 36 x 10 inches
Lent by Robert and Toni Gordon,
Bethesda, Maryland

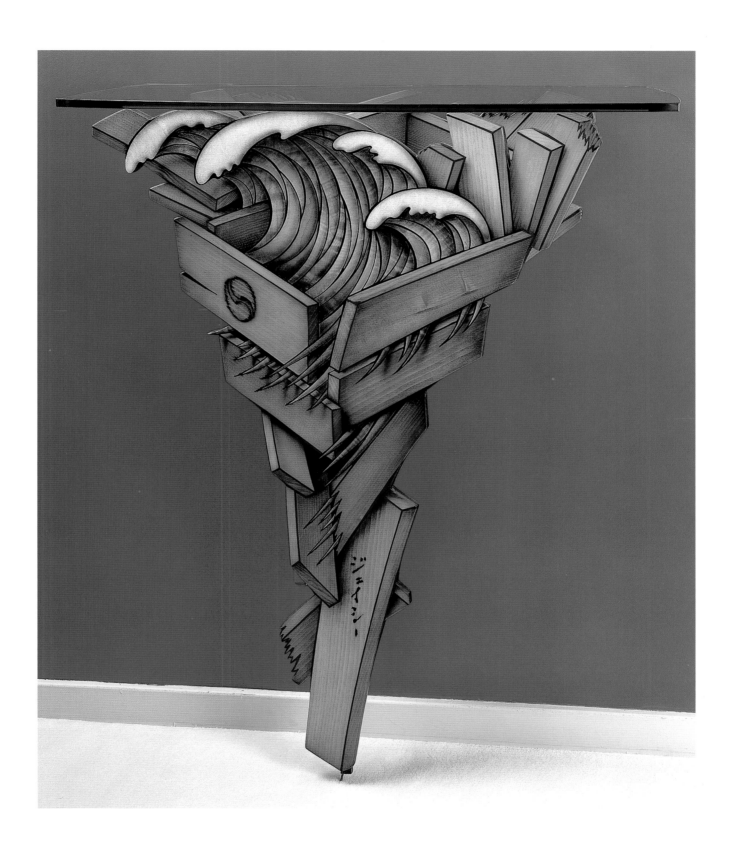

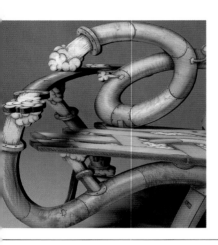

37. steaming poodle bench, 1994–95

Baltic birch plywood, poplar, maple,
Sitka spruce, epoxy resin inlay, aniline dye
31 x 52 x 28 inches
Collection of Oakland Museum of California,
Gift of the Reichel Fund

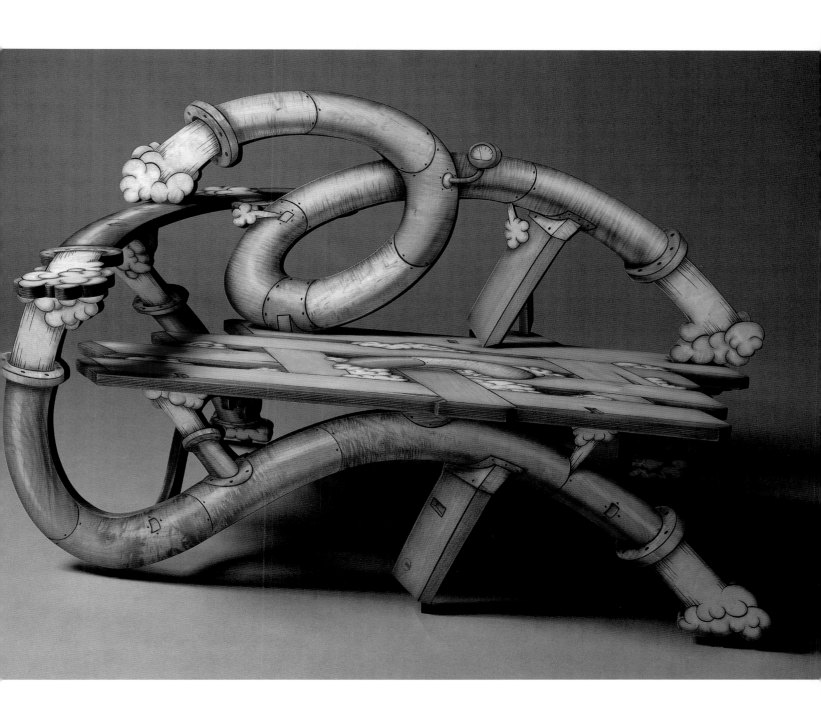

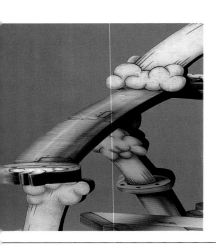

38. steaming poodle chair, 1994–95

Baltic birch plywood, poplar, maple,
Sitka spruce, epoxy resin inlay, aniline dye
30 x 39 x 28 inches
Lent by Arlene and Harvey Caplan,
Short Hills, New Jersey

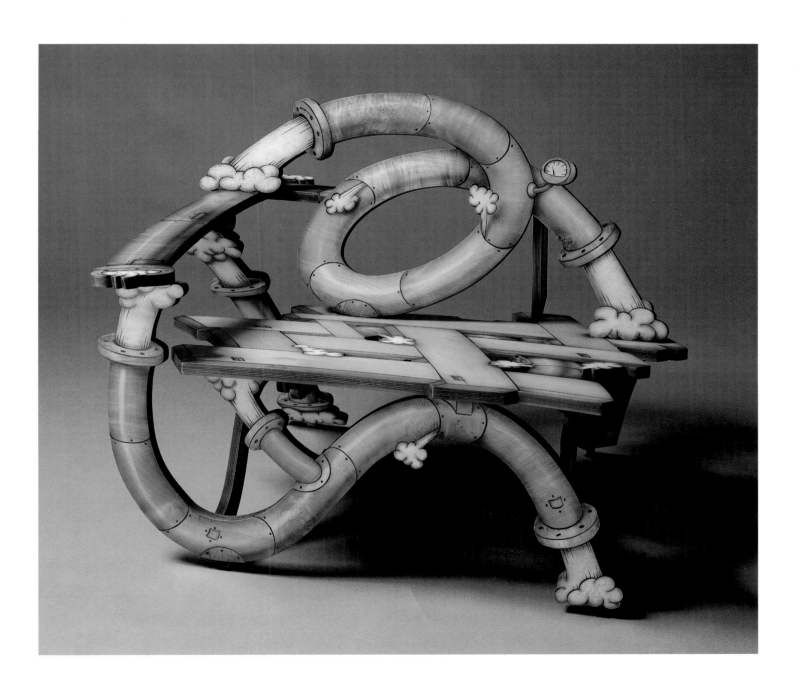

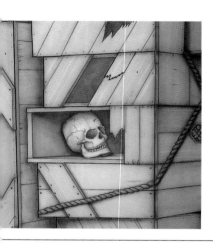

39. cajón de los muertos, 1995
Baltic birch plywood, Sitka spruce, maple, aniline dye,
epoxy resin inlay, metal hardware
85 x 45 x 14 inches
Lent by John W. and Marilyn L. Barrett,
Bethesda, Maryland

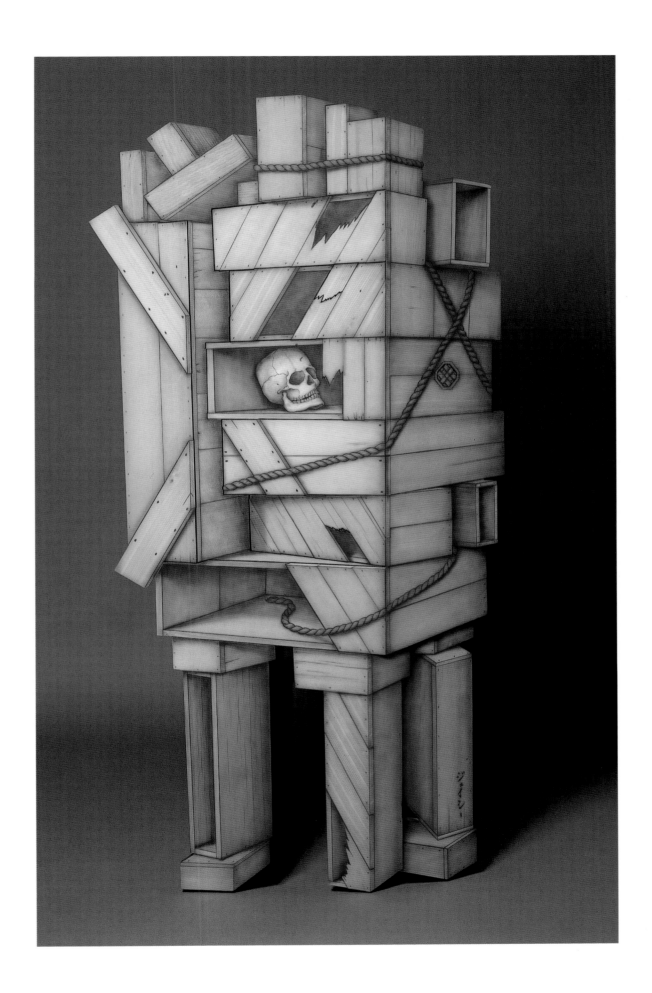

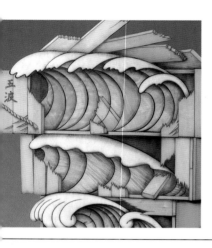

40. how to wrap five waves, 1995

Baltic birch plywood, maple, Sitka spruce,
epoxy resin inlay, oil-based lithography inks,
metal hardware
74 x 46 x 14 inches
Daphne Farago Collection,
Little Compton, Rhode Island

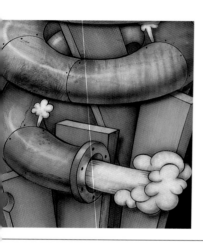

41. steamer chest III, 1995

Baltic birch plywood, basswood, alder, poplar,
maple, epoxy resin inlay, aniline dye, metal hardware
71 x 39 x 18 inches
Lent by Sydney and Frances Lewis

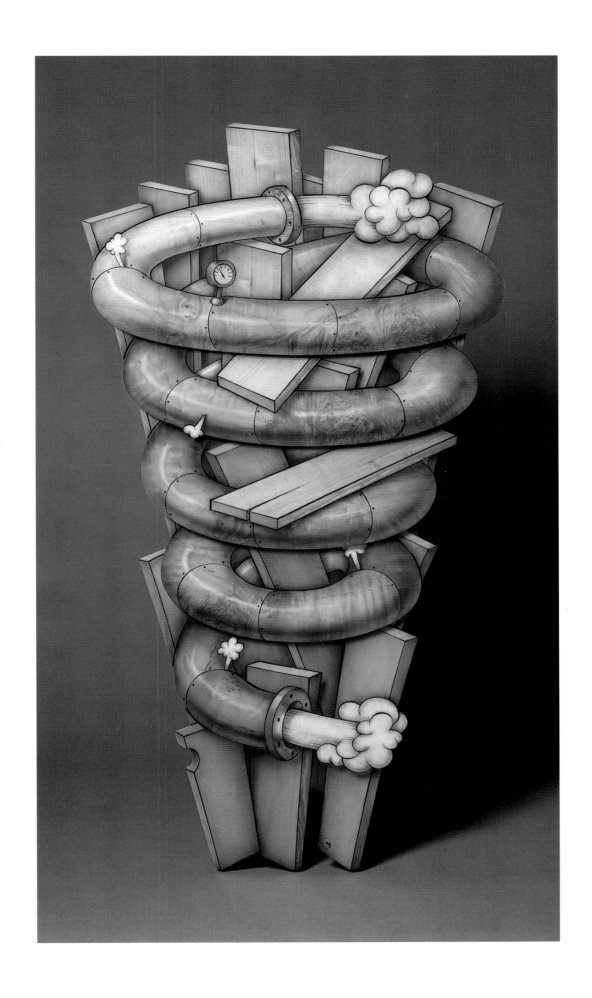

42. tsawnami, 1995

Baltic birch plywood, maple, gum,
Sitka spruce, epoxy resin inlay, aniline dye
79 x 38 x 16 inches
Collection of Albert and Anita Waxman

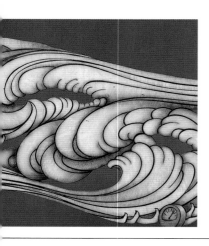

43. when machines
dream of hokusai, 1995

Baltic birch plywood, maple, poplar,
epoxy resin inlay, aniline dye,
oil-based lithography inks, metal hardware
64 x 61 x 2 ½ inches
Lent by Robert and Gayle Greenhill,
Greenwich, Connecticut

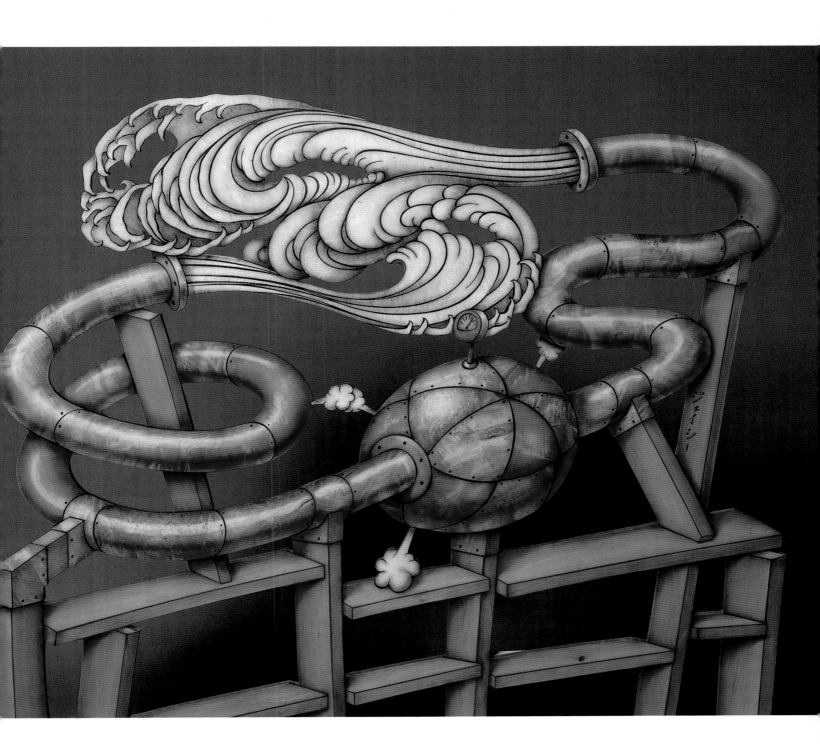

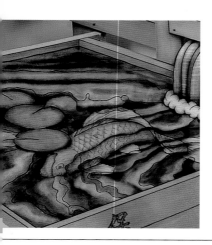

44. conservation, 1996

Baltic birch plywood, Sitka spruce, cherry,
maple, aniline dye, epoxy resin inlay, glass
45 x 95½ x 14½ inches
Lent by Marc and Diane Grainer,
Falls Church, Virginia

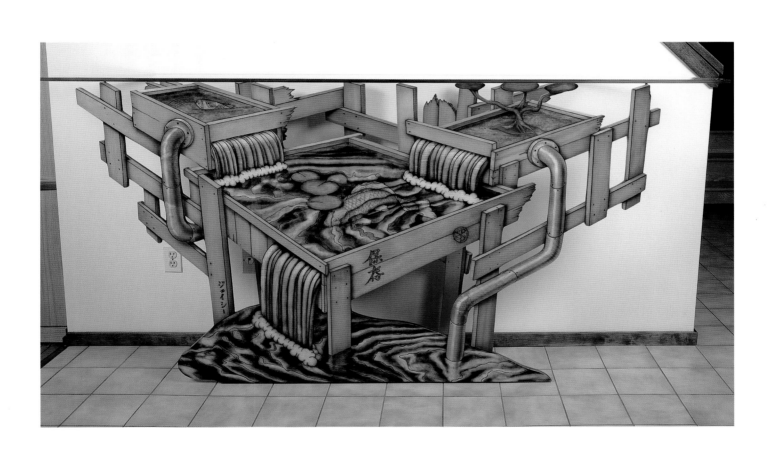

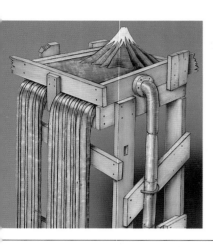

45. conservation bench, 1997

Baltic birch plywood, Sitka spruce, cherry, maple,
epoxy resin inlay, oil-based lithography inks, aniline dye
49 x 68 x 30 inches
Lent by Colleen and John Kotelly,
Washington, D.C.

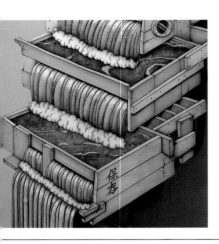

46. conservation chest I, 1997

Baltic birch plywood, Sitka spruce, maple, cherry,
epoxy resin inlay, oil-based lithography inks,
aniline dye, metal hardware
75 x 59 x 14 inches
Lent courtesy of Mitchell Berliner Collection

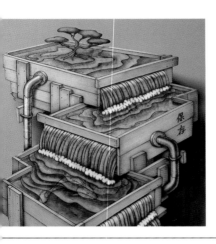

47. conservation chest II, 1997

Baltic birch plywood, Sitka spruce, maple, epoxy resin inlay,
oil-based lithography inks, aniline dye, metal hardware
79 x 42 x 14 inches
John W. and Marilyn L. Barrett,
Bethesda, Maryland

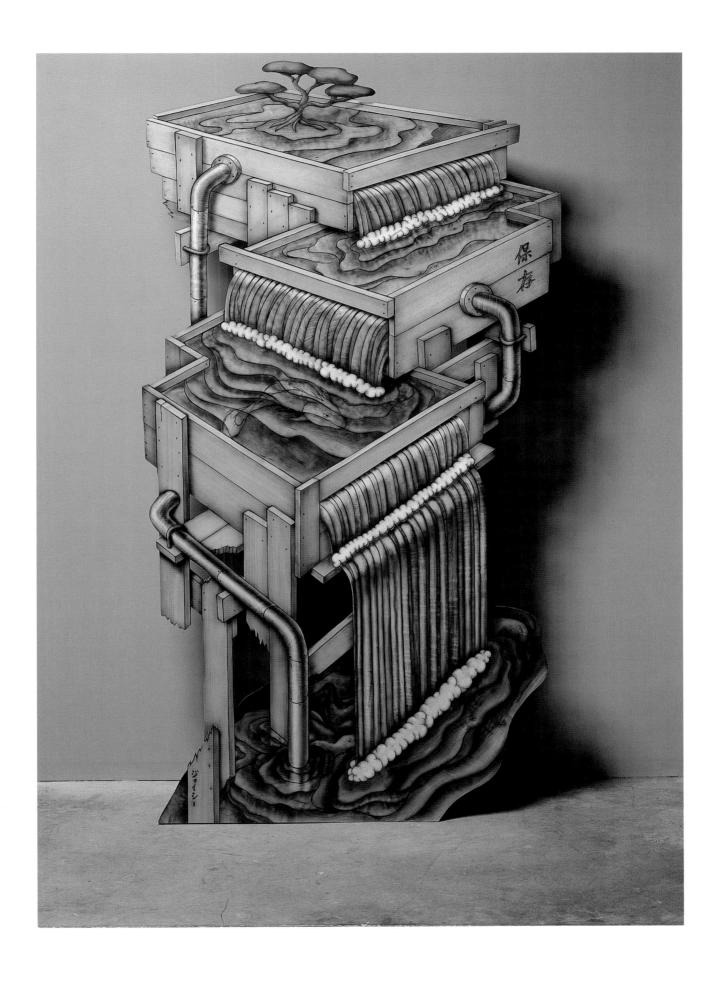

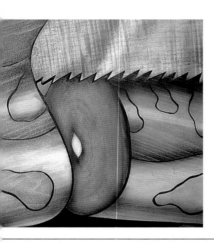

48. road to dreamland, 1997

Baltic birch plywood, gum, maple, poplar,
epoxy resin inlay, aniline dye, metal hardware
60 x 83 x 3 inches
Lent courtesy Franklin Parrasch Gallery, New York

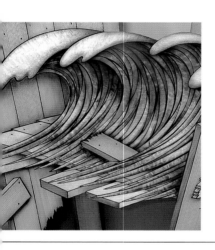

49. saw wave, 1997
Baltic birch plywood, Sitka spruce,
maple, glass, epoxy resin inlay,
oil-based lithography inks,
aniline dye, metal hardware
41 x 65 x 10 inches
Lent courtesy Franklin Parrasch Gallery,
New York

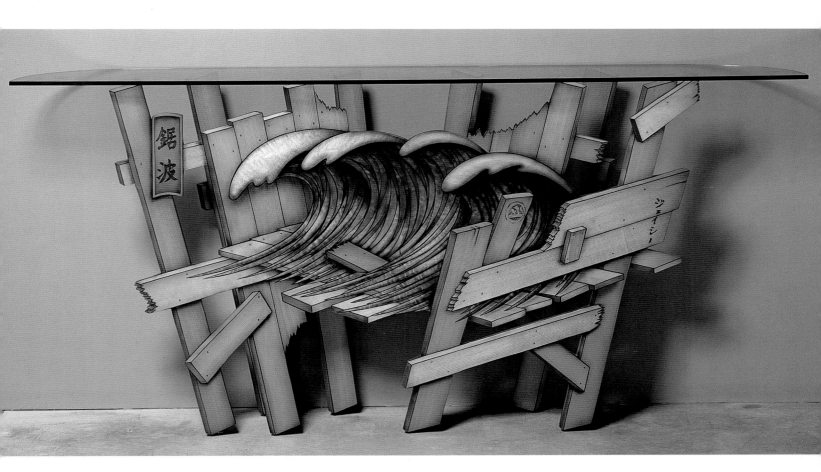

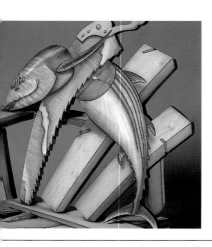

50. sashimi side chair, 1997
Baltic birch plywood, poplar, maple,
epoxy resin inlay, oil-based lithography inks, aniline dye
41 x 29 x 29 inches
Lent by Sylvia and Eric Elsesser,
Sausalito, California

biography

1946   John Carl Cederquist born August 7 in Altadena, California, to Kenneth and Lillian Cederquist.

1963   Graduates from Covina High School, Covina, California.

1964   Attends Long Beach State College (now California State University, Long Beach) so he can pursue his passion for surfing while studying art. Starting out as a graphic design major, by junior year decides to switch to crafts. Begins carving and working with wood. Encouraged by a friend to consider a career teaching crafts at the college level.

1969   Receives B.A. in art from Long Beach State. On August 10 marries Suzanne Marie Patry, whom he met while both were studying art at Long Beach State. The couple settles in Long Beach.

1971   December 29, their daughter, Tera Cederquist, is born in Long Beach.

1971   Receives M.A. from Long Beach State and participates in masters' show. Soon after, shows small, wall-mounted cabinet pieces that include tubular shapes of formed leather at Gallery del Sol in Santa Barbara. The cabinets incorporate carving, lathe turning, laminating, and other woodworking techniques. Pieces are partly influenced by the industrial refinery area in Long Beach, where he saw "steam, smoke, and thousands of tubes going everywhere . . . there was always something venting off steam or a big flame." Also shows leather boxes in *Design XI* at the Pasadena Art Museum, Pasadena, an exhibition of craft items, jewelry, and furniture and industrial design.

1972   Teaches crafts at California State University, at both Long Beach and Los Angeles campuses.

1973   Moves with family to Costa Mesa. Teaches three-dimensional design at California State University, Fullerton.
Begins work on "Michelin Man" series, which occupies him until 1979. In this series, he combines leather-formed, balloon-tire shapes with circular wooden elements to create jewelry cabinets. The wood elements in these pieces are radically curved. Looking for ways to make them structurally sound, he laminates solid wood onto the face of plywood. This technical solution leads him to the discovery that he can create illusionistic images by cutting, gluing, and painting the solid wood veneer in ways that resemble woodblock prints.

1974   Exhibits leather-formed pieces in *Coffins and Cradles*, The Craft and Folk Art Museum, Los Angeles. Exhibits a bentwood-style rocking chair in *Chairs in Motion*, California State University, Fullerton.

1975   Accepts position as art instructor at Saddleback Community College, Mission Viejo, California. Receives Individual Fellowship from the National Endowment for the Arts. Meets the renowned English woodworker John Makepeace, who invites him to give workshop on leather forming at Parnham, Makepeace's school in Beaminster, England.

1976   Moves with family to Capistrano Beach. Buys a house, converting a garage to use as a studio. Participates in three exhibitions: *California Design '76*, Pasadena Museum of Art, Pasadena (catalogue published); *California Craftsman*, Monterey Peninsula Museum of Art, Monterey; and *American Crafts '76: An Esthetic View*, Museum of Contemporary Art, Chicago. Begins teaching at Saddleback Community College, where he continues to teach today.

1977   Chosen to be a member of the National Endowment for the Arts' Selection Panel.

1978   Gives second workshop at Beaminster, England. Has a solo exhibition of formed-leather and wood pieces at Parnham House, Dorset, England.

1979   Shows in three exhibitions: *Our Own Artists*, Newport Harbor Museum, Newport Beach, California, and Museum of Art, Carnegie Institute, Pittsburgh; *Art in Modern Handcrafts*, Herbert F. Johnson Museum of Art, Cornell University, Ithaca, New York; and *New Handmade Furniture*, The Museum of Contemporary Crafts, New York. Grows disenchanted with wood and formed-leather pieces. While teaching two- and three-dimensional design at Saddleback, becomes interested in perspective and the relationship between two and three dimensions, illusion and reality, object and image. Watching *Popeye* cartoons with Tera, begins photographing them with 35mm slides and studying the drawing. Begins thinking about "a new genre of furniture in the cartoons, much more fluid, much more alive. I'm trying to figure out how I can exist in two worlds, how I can make this work in two worlds." Makes a simple side table to test his theories, constructing it in what he calls "two-and-a-half dimensions."

1980   Exhibits a bentwood-style rocking chair in *California Woodworking*, The Oakland Museum, Oakland (catalogue published).
Throughout the 1980s, bases pieces on designs for bentwood furniture from a reprint of a Michael Thonet catalogue. Plays with technique and illusion. Chairs look real when viewed from the correct point of view, but are distorted from any other point of view.

1981   Makes a table, *First Piece*. It is the first time he successfully combines two and three dimensions in one piece.
Included in exhibition *Made in L.A.: Contemporary Crafts '81, a Bicentennial Celebration*, The Craft and Folk Art Museum, Los Angeles (catalogue published).

1982   Creates pivotal piece in the new cartoon style, *Olive's Chair*, inspired by a chair in the cartoon character Olive Oyl's living room.

1983   Takes a sabbatical from Saddleback Community College. Produces work for a solo exhibition, *John Cederquist: Deceptions*, The Craft and Folk Art Museum, Los Angeles (catalogue published). This work is crucial for his development. He begins making absolutely flat, illusionistic chests of drawers.

1984   Begins making functional furniture and starts creating original imagery to accommodate this. Makes *Auntie Macasser Goes West*, which is later purchased by the Oakland Museum. Adds more rooms to his home, doing his own construction. Participates in *Material Evidence: Master Craftsmen Explore Colorcore*, Workbench: The Gallery, New York, and Renwick Gallery, National Museum of American Art, Smithsonian Institution, Washington, D.C.

1985   Collector Ronald Abramson, a Washington, D.C., lawyer, begins buying pieces in advance, based solely on drawings.

1986   Shows work in *Craft Today—the Poetry of the Physical*, American Craft Museum, New York (traveling exhibition; catalogue published). Receives second Individual Fellowship from the National Endowment for the Arts.

1988   Participates in exhibition *Trompe-l'Oeil: The Magic of Deception*, Muckenthaller Cultural Center, Fullerton, California. Begins making functional chests of drawers that look like stacked crates. Trompe-l'oeil images create the illusion that the viewer can see the contents of the crates.

1989   Participates in *New American Furniture: The Second Generation of Studio Furnituremakers*, Museum of Fine Arts, Boston (traveling exhibition; catalogue published). Artists are invited to create works inspired by furniture in the museum's collection. Makes *Le Fleuron Manquant (The Missing Finial)*, an illusionistic tour de force in which pieces of an ornate highboy appear to be packed, impossibly, in a stack of wooden crates.
        Hires Chris LaBonte, a former student and highly skilled craftsman. LaBonte's expertise in handling the technical demands of producing the pieces leaves Cederquist free to create more work.

1990   Joins Franklin Parrasch Gallery, New York, and is shown in Parrasch's *Circa 1990* show. Work is reviewed by the *New York Times*, *Art and Antiques*, *Sculpture* magazine, *Elle*, and other publications. Still a passionate surfer, becomes interested in creating pieces with waves crashing through them. Makes *Tubular*, the first such work, with waves inspired by woodblock prints by Hokusai.

1991   Exhibits at Franklin Parrasch Gallery, New York (catalogue published) and, through the gallery, the Chicago International New Art Forms Exposition, Chicago. Work is reviewed in *Art in America* and other publications. Moves studio from garage to larger studio workspace in San Clemente.

1992   Included in two exhibitions at the Franklin Parrasch Gallery, New York: *California Dreaming* and *The Endowed Chair* (catalogue published for the latter).

1993   Has solo exhibition at the Franklin Parrasch Gallery, New York (catalogue published). Included in five group exhibitions: *Inaugural Exhibition of the Daphne Farago Wing*, Rhode Island School of Design, Museum of Art, Providence; *California Dreaming— Revisited*, Franklin Parrasch Gallery, New York; *Visions Reflected*, The Sybaris Gallery, Royal Oak, Michigan; *Transcending Boundaries*, Elsa Mott Ives Gallery, 53rd Street YWCA, New York; and *Material Vision: Image and Object*, Tarble Arts Center, Eastern Illinois University, Charleston (catalogue essay for the last by Matthew Kangas).

1994   Work included in *SOFA Exposition,* Chicago, and *Tenth Anniversary Exhibition,*
         Albers Fine Art Gallery, Memphis, Tennessee.

1995   Solo exhibition at Franklin Parrasch Gallery, New York (catalogue published). Show
         is reviewed by Roberta Smith in the *New York Times.*
         Now making furniture incorporating images of tubes with steam blasting out ends
         and seams, including *Steaming Poodle Bench, Steamer Chest III,* and *Steaming
         Poodle Chair.* Steam patterns are based on Hokusai prints of whirlpools, epitomized
         by *When Machines Dream of Hokusai,* the headboard of a bed with tubes emitting
         steam in the shape of waves.

1996   Gives lecture and workshop at the Philbrook Art Center in Tulsa, Oklahoma. Is included
         in two exhibitions: *Form over Function: Late-Twentieth-Century Furniture from the
         Sydney and Frances Lewis Collection,* Marsh Art Gallery, University of Richmond,
         Virginia; and *Tenth Anniversary Show,* Franklin Parrasch Gallery.

1997   Included in *Celebrating American Craft,* Danish Museum of Decorative Art,
         Copenhagen. Has solo exhibition at Franklin Parrasch Gallery, New York. Oakland
         Museum of California solo exhibition, *The Art of John Cederquist: Reality of Illusion*
         (traveling exhibition; catalogue published), opens in September.

selected bibliography

Baker, Kenneth. "Show Emphasizes Utility vs. Aesthetics." *San Francisco Chronicle,* March 31, 1991, p. 35.

Belvin, Marjory E. *Design through Discovery.* New York: Holt, Rinehart and Winston Publishers, 1976.

California Design '76. Exh. cat. Pasadena, Calif.: Pasadena Museum of Art, 1976.

California Woodworking. Exh. cat. Oakland, Calif.: The Oakland Museum, 1980.

Clements, Paul. "High-Craft Homage: New American Furniture Reinvents Its Past." *Museum & Arts Washington,* May–June 1990, p. 74.

Conway, Patricia. *Art for Everyday.* New York: Clarkson Potter Publishers, 1990.

Cooke, Edward S., Jr. *New American Furniture: The Second Generation of Studio Furniture-makers.* Exh. cat. Boston: Museum of Fine Arts, 1989.

Danto, Arthur C. *The Endowed Chair.* Exh. cat. New York: Franklin Parrasch Gallery, 1992.

_____. "Furniture as Art." *Nation,* April 23, 1990, pp. 571–75.

_____. "Master of Illusion: Furniture Maker John Cederquist Sets Traps for the Eye." *House & Garden,* December 1996, pp. 50–53.

Emanuelli, Sharon. *John Cederquist: Deceptions.* Exh. cat. Los Angeles: The Craft and Folk Art Museum, 1983.

Jones, Ronald. "I'm Confused." In *John Cederquist.* Exh. cat. New York: Franklin Parrasch Gallery, 1993.

Joyce, Earnest. *Encyclopedia of Furniture Making.* New York: Sterling Publishing Co., 1987.

Kangas, Matthew. *Material Vision: Image and Object.* Exh. cat. Charleston: Tarble Arts Center, Eastern Illinois University, 1993.

Koplos, Janet, "John Cederquist at Franklin Parrasch." *Art in America 79* (October 1991): 156.

Made in L.A.: Contemporary Crafts '81, a Bicentennial Celebration. Exh. cat. Los Angeles: The Craft and Folk Art Museum, 1981.

Manhart, Marcia, and Tom Manhart, eds. *The Eloquent Object: The Evolution of American Art in Craft Media since 1945.* Exh. cat. Tulsa, Okla.: Philbrook Museum of Art, 1987.

Parrasch, Franklin. *John Cederquist.* Exh. cat. New York: Franklin Parrasch Gallery, 1991.

_____. "The Unreliable Narrator: John Cederquist." In *John Cederquist.* Exh. cat. New York: Franklin Parrasch Gallery, 1995.

Schofield, Maris. *Decorative Art and Modern Interiors.* London: Studio Vista, 1975.

Slesin, Suzanne. "Currents: Furniture Designers' Rebirth." *New York Times,* January 4, 1990, p. C11.

_____. "Furniture as Fine Sculpture." *New York Times,* May 10, 1990, p. B6.

Smith, Karen Sandra. "The Art of the Illusion." *Art of California,* November 1992, pp. 52–53.

Smith, Paul J., and Edward Lucie-Smith. *Craft Today—the Poetry of the Physical.* New York: Weidenfeld and Nicolson Publishers, 1986.

Smith, Roberta. "John Cederquist." Art in Review, *New York Times,* April 28, 1995, p. 34.

Stapleton, Constance. "The New Art Furniture: Challenging the Boundaries between Art and Craft." *Sculpture,* July–August 1990, pp. 35–39.

Updike, John. "Put-Ons and Take-Offs: Contemporary Furniture that Parodies or Pays Homage to the Classics." *Art & Antiques,* February 1990, pp. 70–75, 104.